We still don't know exactly what happened
on the evolutionary arc
that launched humans into the stratosphere
and left the others far behind.
It's wonderful being human.

Two Thin Lines

Alexandra K. Corbin

Published by Red Roof Publishing,
An imprint of Small New York, LLC,
Beekman, New York 12570 and
Brooklyn, New York 11231

First printing 2018

CONTENTS

Now the First Words

I am an artist and always have been. But over the years I have become extremely perplexed, even frustrated, because I realized that 'Art' really does not have boundless creative opportunities. In fact, there appeared to be rather stubborn protocols of image-crafting that prohibited willy-nilly expression. For example, a mark placed even slightly at a greater distance and at a certain angle from another one mysteriously interferes with an intended perception. This is why I call this small book, 'Two Thin Lines'. At what point does the placement of two thin lines predict a recognizable outcome like a triangle or a deer's head and at what point in their contextual arrangement does it fail to suggest anything at all?

We attribute 'talent' to those rare people who are conversant with the vagaries of these protocols and usually for having highly skilled drafting abilities. Highly skilled draftsmen, however, are not at all any kind of measure for deep knowledge about these things. Ancient artists, cartoonists, New Guinea tribesmen, boundless artisans of all stripes and levels of skill - are conversant with their specialty of protocols. But what is it, really?

Over the past thirty years there has been a gigantic degree of attention and research in the neuro-psychology field devoted to this curious object lexicon. On the surface, we seem to inherit a sensitivity for these formulae, if you will, either innately or as a matter of course through culture and personal experience. Both are contributors. The result of that sensitivity is called 'recognition'. A very apt word because it really means re-cognitizing a slurry of inputs into reliable formations. There is a system to it though it is not absolutely universal because culture and personality and life history do tweak it considerably. Common sense underscores whatever universality there is to it is based on psychological sensitivity for the behavioral salience of things. As long as the process stays in our heads, it is pure cognition.

All of which makes sense since we spend so much of our daily lives trying to break recognition down and then reconstruct it to suit our fancy and activate it in a variety of physical and behavioral modes that allow us to predict outcomes for which we are individually on the lookout. For those who are always trying to lose weight, for example, they constantly consider the widths between things like chairs at restaurants and between cars not to mention clothes on a rack, in order to determine if they can shimmy their bodies into, between and among. An extremely skinny person's notion of a restaurant aisle varies from that of someone else.

Therefore, their cognition or mental assessing of their world - has a distinct partiality for what a decent size space between things feels like which is inevitably based on their own body size and extrapolated forward. Children obsess over the motion and general appearance of a nurturer's eyes to predict whether they will be embraced, fed, scolded or carried. Upside down and right side up, they are far more sensitive to the prosody of the eyes and can read faces both ways, something that older children and adults simply cannot do. But eyes, in general, are the key predictor of intra-social behavior and are universal icons for this reason.

A lot of what can plainly be called a cognitive obsession has to do with our primitive compulsion to spot things ever faster and faster by means of generalizing. Each of us does this in order to accept which notions in the form of sounds, shapes, colors, etc. are personally more affective, alluring or atypical than the commonplace, a good deal of which is guided by culture. It makes our ability to navigate our world that much more efficient. Long, long, ago, some people, perhaps shamans or perhaps those who simply loved doing it and studying with the masters in ancient ateliers, seem to have been more acutely aware with that dynamic object lexicon and felt a need to publish it. In fact, that is precisely what made them art practitioners. James Abbott MacNeil Whistler the 19th century American painter would agree, "Nature…sings her exquisite song to the artist alone."

Remarkably, the idioms of these basic constructs have not changed that much. This book is about how it 'got writ' in the first place. We discuss the neural area called Brodmann 44, 45 or Broca's Area as well as the rather curious proximity of other keys neurons lodged around the Sylvian fissure.

*

I say 'dynamic' object lexicon because of the force of its impact and how it guides us in all matters of perception. Often the term 'dynamic' suggests that the thing itself changes considerably over time as is the case with contemporary art which consciously tries its best to disrupt the old habits. But it actually just reinvents them. We simply cannot manage to discard the hard-wired salience of basic attributes. For example, which facial feature can we more easily discard without losing the sense of a face; a nose, a mouth or the eyes? We all know the answer to that so have eons of others. You can discard the nose and/or the mouth, just never the eyes.

I had a sneaky feeling that understanding why we are still displaying 'hands' in clusters just as the cavemen did, might bear witness to this peculiar thing we call 'recognition' in its most primal form. There had to be both impulsive as well as compulsive psychological motives for stamping the relief of one's hand in mud or dipping it in paint and slapping it onto rock faces or apartment walls as I did at age three. Or casting them in plastic and stuffing them into boxes and then displaying this 'art' for hundreds of thousands of dollars in fancy galleries.

Yes, they are funny and fascinating extensions of ours and certainly this has impact on our love of them. But the universal sameness and durability of these imprints strongly suggest that the urge had to have started as a cognitive parsing instinct. The logical reason likely having to do with understanding them as a possession and ultimately as manifestations of oneself. And why not celebrate these multi-motile extremities? After all, our hands are rather helpful appendages, necessities of survival for grasping and stroking and probing and bracing us against falling, to name a few of its remarkable attributes.

More wonderful is the entertainment value of just watching one hand or even one finger doing something completely different than the others. Babies are onto to this at four months old as they coo their way into vocalizing at the same time. You see them in the strollers multi-tasking as they explore all the new things they own. They are shuttling between early language instincts and looking at their hands and holding their feet in similar possessive ways. They are figuring out what controls these things by virtue of controlling these things that are always in their field of vision. In this fashion they are figuring out what objects in the world belong exclusively to them.

Early on, arms and legs might have been perceived as tentacled extensions like those of other animals. Who really knows. Oddly enough, the free-standing handprint seems to have become the real mystery as do all things that exist outside of us so that the roiling question about identity swiftly became, "Is that smudge I made the same thing as me?" When we owned the activity, we owned the investiture of self with the mark we made as a unique representation in short form of an individual. Transferring value to an abstract shape (or tone) is about systematic coding. And systematic coding is the same thing a cognition. The cognitive habit once it began, could never be stopped.

These hand images addressed and still do address, two universally conflicting concerns of every human being; that of wanting to be certain we are a normal member of the species but only to a point. That toxic power struggle between the need for individuality versus commonality obviously drives the selfie epidemic which is precisely why it is an epidemic. We are that needy and still that confused. It is also likely that the selfsame frustration propelled the hand print manifestation for upward of almost 100,000 years. It could have been much longer and much more pervasive. We only 'recently' found more stable places for their display when we found caves could be permanent shrines.

From understanding that we self-manifested in sounds and motions and marks, we quickly designated them as decisive. From 'decisive' we needed to build in a system of meaning and equations around both the doing of it as well as the things themselves that we left for done. We could revisit them because they now had a physical location and we could repeat them through like actions. Why did we need to extrapolate meaning? Because the new neurons in our brains and their routing of signals determined it be so.

Then came the discovery that 'publishing' itself as a means to make some part of yourself visible over and over to your conspecifics as well as yourself - held a tremendous power of persuasion. The self-identifying image could be manipulated, organized, re-produced, shared, altered and made into a pattern. We wanted this very multisensory activity, not just the static 3d image but the chain linked operation of motion and touch involved in making it, to sear itself into our long-term memories. For some reason it was very important because the linkage of events leading to the final image was an essential part of the story and the essence of 'meaning'. It became a kind of baseline or background against which the drama of daily life was played out: "As I was stamping my hand in the wet ochre, a huge rat ran by and the print was a blob." That blob becomes the place holder for a recounting of the event. A story is made, a memory and a symbol all at once.

All this identity thinking and self-research had to have been prefigured by the cognition protocols of identity. Finding out what resides in our brains that always seeks what 'identity' is in the first place, is precisely where one has to begin the search for 'recognition' protocols and not in the visual system or peri visual system. Only from there can we then proceed with the incredible adventure of outwardly replicating aspects of ourselves and then on and on to practically every aspect of our species-specific environment. Once we get the rhythm of this method by practicing on ourselves, applying it to other things is simple.

Right here, at this juncture, wherein the need to correlate identity as a collection of (our) many parts, is ground zero for the great evolutionary conundrum of what separated us from the other experiments in hominins. This is that gigantic leaping forward that took place in our species. What growth of new neurons and the layered compacting of them in specific hubs caused these personality changes and impulses in haptic industry to make things. How did we get from waving our hands in front of our noses as infants to the notion of ourselves as a unique and stable collection of physical appurtenances? And then to an indefatigable passion for identifying other aspects of the environment in a similar fashion?

This was and still is about the master control of our limbs and body in space and time by acknowledging a separation of powers; that a certain part of our body summarizes the collection into a unity and sends the orders for the motor system to execute them. With this came an understanding of a strange phenomenon that stretched our cognitive powers to that of profound conceptual complexity and tremendous empowerment.

These were the revelations that the undersides or printed sides of our hands which clearly looked different were also the mirror or horizontal flip of the outer side and that all of it belonged to 'us'. Indeed, a rather befuddling collection. This concept of 'collection' is something all animals share to a degree and this is where we have to begin our research. Instead of worms and dried grass for nests, we began to collect sounds, words, gestures, people, places and things. Then families, tribes, communities and rival communities and with that, of course, a host of far more complicated things.

*

There are days when faced with a blank page, so to speak, that I wonder how to get beyond the triangle and the circle shapes and swirls that make up our basic shape palette. For these are universal absolutes in human design. Often, I wonder if there is something else out there, some shapes that we have never ever accessed the reason being that I cannot invent what is beyond my sensory ken. Might I have read my 'umwelt' or my species' idiosyncratic world differently if I had a visual system that transferred light quanta into amorphous colors instead of tilting lines? Or been endowed with just one more color sensor than the three we must live with?

*

Some manner of hominins had already managed for millions of years to identify as 'oneself' their collective physical parts. We see this in the gaited placement of their steps directly into the footprints of what they 'thought' was some other conspecific's. This evidence is suggested by the famous Laetoli footsteps of Tanzania near Olduvai Gorge discovered by Mary Leakey around 1976.

This lucky find is seminal because it is clear evidence that some distant relative absorbed as tacitly reliable that our hands belong to us as well as our feet and those other 'things' that always seemed to come along for the ride everywhere we looked and everywhere we turned. This collection we recognized as 'me'. And from there, we noticed the similarities of other shapes and especially other moving things and determined these were 'you' and those were 'it'. We had to have invented paradigms for searching and paradigms of likeness and difference in order to place our feet in a like shaped footprint belonging to others. It is one of the favorite first games of a child.

From there we could predict from abstractions what regularly occurring shapes augured ominous events which we wanted nothing of and which were altogether benign. These entities all of which were collections of salient parts in their own right, became the parables of daily living encapsulated in static form. It is still how we take note of danger and safety. How we nurture our young and how wisdom was and is conveyed across tribes, across water, across land and across time.

In order to pass around and to publish the knowledge of what is significant first to ourselves - so we always remember - and then to others so they take it as gospel, we recorded that significance in regularly occurring notations. These are the recognition patterns we use and have used since that quirky alteration in our brains took place hundreds of thousands and likely millions of years ago.

Alexandra K. Corbin
Brooklyn, NY 2018

Two Thin Lines

My first day in Theodore Gaster's comparative religion course at Columbia University was quite the eye opener then and more so now given the distance I have traveled. For one thing, I was unprepared for his height, nor his super-erect strut in which he kicked out his feet like oversized flippers. Nor was I prepared for his deeply marinated British accent stubbornly steeped in clips and cadences despite four decades in the United States.

He had a tiny, sharp nose but an enormous towering forehead, beautiful long fingers, and full lips, with dimples that he used to great effect when hitting the punch line. It was clear from the moment he made his dramatic entrance and embarked on his romp across the record of human neediness for comfort through ritual, that I would switch out of my intended major. Dressed in an expertly tailored British pinstriped blue suit, China white cotton shirt, and crimson Peruvian tie, he clopped pigeon toed straight over to the blackboard and slowly, if you can believe this was possible, drew two thin lines converging in a point. Then he waited a beat before luxuriously finishing off the drawing with a bottom line connecting the other two.

'Can some brave soul kindly tell me what this is?'
　　He was kidding, right? Even a reasonably well-trained
　　chimp had enough words to come up with the answer.
　　Despite suspecting his ruse, one lone soul couldn't resist taking
　　the bait;
'Maybe a triangle?'
'Incorrect,' he boomed! 'This…,' he tapped the board with the chalk,
　　the white dust sputtering over his gracile fingers and stark dark
　　jacket.
'This is a picture *about* a triangle. It is not a triangle.'
News to all of us smarties.

He continued devouring every dramatic moment like it was his last meal on earth; 'And in the same way, we don't know God, we only know *about* God. That is all we are capable of doing.'
Made sense, where do I sign up.
'Stop scribbling,' he snapped with a bit of a lisp and maybe a tad of spittle jettisoning forth. 'This won't be on a test. It *'tis* a fact of living.'
And then, as if this weren't frightening enough for freshmen on their first day, he added,
'Those of you who do not understand right now what I am saying had best drop this course…NOW!'

***

I did not because I could not. It was obviously far too obvious. I felt at home.

Just now, just as I relate this to you, all of those ripe details hurtle back to me from the deep past, though I am suspicious of how accurate they are. I remember in the movie *Gigi*, Maurice Chevalier warbled, 'Ah yes, I remember it well…' as he charmingly misremembers every single detail of his romance with his old flame Hermione Gingold, who corrects him every step of the way down memory lane.

So, no doubt this recollection of my first brush with comparative religion is some mix of false and true. But there is far more about the impact of this triangle, sitting up there on the board, that keeps me coming back. There was a moment that jelled it all for me, where the excitement of discovery contained within an entertaining scene somehow connected viscerally. It was theater and concept that I decided was a truism, though it might very well have been, and could still certainly be, a matter of my pure conjecture.

That 'Eureka' moment happened when he ever so slowly drew the wobbly third line to close the form of the triangle as if for the first time. What had been a fey picture of an inverted 'V' became something altogether different. Right then, I could feel myself drawing the wobbly line too. Eventually, maybe seconds or years later, I can't really be sure, the story of my first excitement over man's need to explain himself in the grand scheme of things became indelibly linked to this single image.

How so?

Because it became a story by way of a tactile process. The lesson he taught about the limits of our perception and the bias to knowing had morphed over time into something even more instructive about our ability to perceive by memorializing through sensations.

***

It is supremely frustrating but utterly remarkable that we do everything by remote control out of a bony control box that sits atop our spinal column. There is virtually no direct way for our brain to know anything whatsoever, only 'about' something by virtue of vibrations and wavelengths. It's our mission control center. And yes, it is that electrical, that remotely controlled, and that quantum based.

Our physical brain is insensate and our 'mind' non-localized. Were we to try to surgically imbed or 'know,' say, a small glass marble, we couldn't manage the task, let alone feel the actual marble. In his book '*Man on His Nature,*' Sir Charles Sherrington grapples with this frustrating disconnect when addressing the attributes of neural cell matter:

> …it is not a 'thing'. It remains without sensual confirmation and remains without it forever…the mind per se cannot play the piano—mind per se cannot move a finger of a hand. The inconsequence staggers us.

Wilder Penfield, an unavoidable reference in any cognition discussion, was an American neurosurgeon practicing in Canada in the 1950s who used this to great advantage when operating on humans without anesthesia so they could chat with him about their reactions to his probing their cerebral cortex with a mild electric pulse. We still don't know what bytes of cerebral information look or really act like, though we know well the general chemical and electrical behaviors of transferring these bits in pathways around the brain.

Nor do we know how these bytes triage themselves into salience versus disposable rubbish. Although there might not be any really true disposable rubbish. That old attic we call our neocortex has an uncanny ability to hoard everything that comes its way. It can be prompted like visiting an old aunt by any passing and obsolete context or surprising trigger; 'My dear, I do believe I have something just like that. Let me go look.' And out she drags some dusty remnant of her past that she hadn't thought of in sixty years. But she did finally think of it, didn't she?

That is if the reference is sufficiently interesting to focus attention. Some suggest that that which decides if it is interesting enough for a good search through all the dusty corners is what we call consciousness.

Were it that simple, none of us could sleep at night with minds racing hither and 'fro'.

***

Not understanding the micro-universe of this organ is part of its charm and challenge. The most up-to-date text books in neuroscience are plagued with a fair number of paragraphs that end with questions like this: 'How each of these [plug in a sub-cortical system] contributes to perception remains an area of active investigation.' Nevertheless, we've come a long way in a relatively short time, especially since George H. W. Bush declared the 1990s to be the 'Decade of the Brain.' And since the visual cortex seems so dominant both in cortical real estate and pathways, it is only natural for many to query how we transduce imagery to plastic form.

I am far more interested in the big bang of compulsion driving the first cognitive mark, when you face a blank canvas or lump of clay, cave wall, mountain overhang, mammoth's tusk, or the side of smooth china cup. Call it the biology of art. And some such as Ellen Dissanayake have coined action terms like 'artify' because they rightly understand it to be an activity like so many others. These are extremely appropriate but much too general, so let's dig a bit further.

***

For this discussion, we must first address the notion of 'self' as a four-dimensional object in space. Why four dimensions? Because the body form occupies three dimensions, but to navigate it, the mind occupies it as the fourth dimension. You can't put the dynamic stuff of the brain in a bottle; it occupies another format entirely other than a physical one, but it is part of the working 'self' complex.

The reason is obvious. Everything we do is self-guiding and something is doing the directing. And the directing mechanism is manipulating an entity we call 'self.' Such has been the world of philosophy but also the world of our constant reality, a challenging and often confusing world when you stop to think about it. It's as incredible as thinking about how you manage to walk by alternating feet. How do we stand up, how do we keep a pace going, navigate the surfaces, and avoid the bumps? When you do stop to think about it, you lose the fluid gate you had previously taken for granted.

The obvious fact we need to recognize first is that whatever is directing 'us' requires constant feedback to navigate our body through space and around other objects. That feedback is provided by our cranial receptors for sensation (i.e., through the eyes, ears, nose, and mouth). But there has to be more. Our 'touch' antennae are most responsible for how we adjust or feel our bodies in space and respond to 'otherness.' And somewhere or somehow that information must find itself molded into clear identification of the personal body/mind proper.

But otherness is a very tricky concept. It can mean recognition of the separation of body from navigator as above, something autists constantly struggle with because it seems so obvious to them. And in the same way but rarely used as a comparison, it is the same separation of navigator from body that occurs when you are trying to learn a new language or sport. Something or someone funnels to your self-navigator the conceptual algorithms for undertaking something new.

More simply, otherness means everything not pertaining to our body, though maybe it is better to say our conscious body profile. Again, and unfortunately, it also means everything also pertaining to our body as if it were just an object—like watching your fingers type. In fact, it *is* *monitoring* a part of your body in every unique frame of vision (e.g., sound and taste too) and every aspect of your daily life, doing strange motions to accomplish things.

For example, as I am writing this thing, I just heard a zipper on someone's bag. But it wasn't a pure sensation of decibels because I heard it with my hands larger than life smack in front of me pounding away on plastic keys at the same time. If I had my eyes closed, I would have felt my legs crossed or my elbow annoying me on the table. The simultaneity of all sensations requires the navigator to make constant decisions about emphasis and attention.

Even worse, one could go crazy with convoluted fine points about where to draw the line that differentiates the extension of a body proper with not a body proper. Let's keep trying to keep it simple, which is something our brain is laboring at every split second. The thing that draws us back from the turgid world of philosophy, and of all the little 'ifs,' 'whys,' and 'buts' and simultaneity of sounds and movements—in other words, of all kinds of boundary vagaries—is our own sensation of touch and motion because it presents a clearer and more urgent present 'present time.'

For touch, the sensors reside most obviously in the tips of our limbs like the soles of our feet, the fingers, and lips. They respond to stimulation in different ways than do the broader expanses of body such as shins and forearms, the broad field of our backs, etc. But these extremities, keyed by their respective joints, do tell us more about motion and vibrations, which are also incredibly significant to interpreting the self in terms of other things.

***

For example, have you ever stopped to think how 'aware' your arm or leg is to your environment? Next time, when you unfurl yourself from the small seat of your car, think about how your leg 'knows' about not hitting the door frame, or how you and an oncoming jogger veer by millimeters to avoid grazing each other. This is called proprioception, comprehending the positioning of your body, or parts thereof, as a distinct, three-dimensional, enclosed volume.

This is essential to both making objects and making art by, in effect, reliving sensations. When we adjust to oncoming joggers, we project their bounded entity/position *vis-à-vis* ours. It seems simple but it's not. The bottom line? We 'act out' the object we aim to delineate from our circumscribed little place, even the oncoming jogger.

The same holds true in art creation, but it is brought forward and center as the single *modus operandi*, the actual tool of such manufacture. This is one reason you often hear art instructors admonishing students to walk around the figure and 'feel it.' Or some like Picasso and his 'bande' in Montmartre circa 1905, endlessly discussing ways to bring the viewer into the canvas itself in a convoluted riddle where he could make the observer rather than the practitioner imagine what it is like to be the object in the painting. Which was imagined by the artist as to what it was for him to be like the object in the first place. Confused?

> Picasso spent long hours alone in his studio. He was
> exploring how far he could take the experiment to position
> or enfold an object in pictorial space in such a way that the
> viewer could 'walk' around it, introducing into the painting
> a sense of time as well as space. (Roe: 2015)

What they worried over is what we still worry over, and that is for the viewer to *sensate* participation in this alternative flat space. Imagination is a robust enterprise and not a flat-footed, unilateral image construct. So it has to be a psychological construct, a trick, a sleight of hand, a tantalizing invitation to gather all your current sensations into a piece of conceptual luggage and take a short trip elsewhere.

When asked to walk around the model or set up - I can assure you - it tends to make matters worse for the poor art student because it gives off far too much information to filter through to a flat concept, and ultimately, image. The act of impersonation requires too much juggling to then whittle and compress down to a flat, captured and unique view. Humans can project just so much and extricate just so much information from it all. As is often stated, we can recall only a maximum of 7 bits of information at a time, and as we return to the flat drawing surface, pencil in hand, and engage with one segment of these visual factoids at a time, we tend to forget the remaining factoids.

What we are left with is rather interesting: a limited sense of knowing 'about' a thing or place or feeling by whatever physical and mental calipers are available to each of us individually. In other words, we tend to reject the list of information points we noticed, like a crescent shape shadow under the shin, and use the mental calipers of acting out the pose even when sitting. We prefer to impersonate rather than make note of.

The reverse is also true, working on a piece of sculpture from an observed object like a live model. The reason is that observation by walking around or touching something in three dimensions is a chain of operations that connects a cascade of flat and segmented perceptions, like speeding up film frames for the general effect and then trying to translate that back into something volumetric that your fingers and arms embrace as a fluid experience. 'Art' is an exercise that makes this very difficult because it makes the 'switch up' very present in our heads. Let me put it another way.

When you fabricate a 3D form, you do so in stages and by degrees of constantly shifting the angle of the object to work it all around and building it up in stages. Yet your concept for it is somehow internalized as a complete and *fait accompli* freestanding volume, something you understand but cannot rotate slowly in your head like a window display. It's a tacit understanding and virtually impossible to access fully. This little game of ours truly hurts the head.

Once again, we perform the best of all tricks. Instead of melding all those angles of 'seeing' into knowing everything possible about that solid form, we just imagine we are that form itself. That means we must impersonate a vase of flowers. Trust me, it works. Just watch the artist. When drawing a tilted head, his tilts. When drawing a rigid back, he straightens his. When drawing flowers, the shoulders feel different, maybe there's a smile on the face. When drawing an angry cat, his mouth tenses. Put electrodes on his shoulders, his cheeks, his scalp, his back. You'd see it then. And when drawing a shrugging shoulder, I lift mine. Want to call it mimicry? Go ahead, but it is mimicry with an added kick.

The fact is that it is a mind divided against itself.

***

'Self-other' is what they commonly call this shift. It is a form of pure imagining that seems to regularly light up specific areas of the brain. It's nice to think that the brain has reserved a reliable place for this 'self-center.' It was initially disclosed as an anecdotal imitation affect such as mirroring others identified as 'like oneself.' And given the close genetic coding with ours of about 93% to 94% likeness, the theory was that if monitoring macaque monkeys saw certain areas 'light up,' it was very likely we had the same mechanics. We had no choice for humanitarian reasons but to experiment with these monkeys instead of the great apes.

Nevertheless, that 6% difference is a vast difference of twenty million years of divergent mechanics and talent. For example, in one voxel or cubic byte seen in an fMRI, there are millions of cells at play. To date we can't drill down on those so we can't identify their functions.

Worse, if Macaques lack cell types common to us such as spindle or Von Economo cells, you are looking at an extremely clumsy alliteration. According to Richard Passingham (2009:6-11), '…there are 'spindle cells' or 'Von Economo neurones' in the anterior cingulate cortex and anterior insula of the human but not macaque brain.' More on this fascinating ACC later.

Further, the Planum Temporale, a part of Wernicke's speech area along the Sylvian Fissure, is the most asymmetrical segment in the human brain, with a variance in size for some of us of up to five times larger for the left hemisphere than the right. Wernicke's is a tricky cluster of neurons that has the ability in us to connect sounds as words without the meaning. Much more study of this neural complex is obviously necessary.

When disconnected from Broca's Area, which helps generate symbolism and therefore meaning, Wernicke's production of jargon seems like an obvious mess of sounds. But the fact that the sounds are still constructed into words is suspiciously interesting in and of itself. Nevertheless, no asymmetry exists in Macaques, though it certainly does for the great apes regardless of their deficiencies in verbal communication.

As technology has permitted, we have 'seen' the voxels of self/otherness cells at work, though again, lacking fine detail. This body of research is vastly complex and particularly significant when studying autistic spectrum disorders. Though given the limitations of functional MRIs and transcranial magnetic stimulation to track specific threads of reactive cells, I suspect transacting self/otherness is a far more pervasive lacework pattern, and far more idiosyncratic. But these intrepid scientists have indeed found certain areas of key interest in the inferior parietal lobe, especially on the right side.

When we speak of self/other in the context of verbalizing, we are speaking of good ole gossiping. Yes, spreading rumors and judging others, being petty, commenting on the physical attributes of others, noticing day-to-day peculiarities, habits, and commonalities. It is our very human way of addressing this idiosyncratic sensitivity for self-otherness. It exercises our individual abilities to be ever-alert about acting like someone or choosing not to act like someone else even as we harp about how cold and rotten our next-door neighbors are, ex-friends, and just better-looking specimens.

***

All of which is wondering what it might be like to be them momentarily. How exactly we perform this 'acting' trick of holding our swarming sensations in abeyance and shifting over to what the object might feel like as a volume in space is a highly sophisticated developmental skill lacking in very young children. The reason is that they are still learning about their new locomotive and navigational skills, about to whom precisely those cute extremities seem to belong. Also, about touching and extension, crawling, walking, and distance. And about falling and pain and trying to gather and coordinate all those flaying parts so there is no further pain or upset. Ages three to four is when they physically integrate all of this knowledge into a comfortable working notion of self.

We think. Personally, I think it's a whole lot earlier. We just lack the means to tease out this information. Around four years old, they begin to flip themselves over mentally and become psychological acrobats. It depends on a familiarity and enjoyment of themselves as a full-blown entity - in other words - as a cognitive icon, meaning who and what they are in their own head. And once an icon, they can finally decide how they choose and where they choose to place their little soldier mini-selves on any map, in a reflection or mirrored map, a room map, a playschool map, any and every kind of social, visual, and spatial map they choose.

Again, autists cannot do this and for those high-performing ones, conceptually positing oneself somewhere else is a very tough row to hoe.

***

If you bear in mind that 'empathy' for all of us is a metaphysical construct, then the 'leap' from iconizing oneself to a Theory of Mind is hardly remarkable. It does suggest it is an acquired skill rather than a genetic trait, the degrees of which are so striking and dissimilar from person to person and definitely from culture to culture. Stories, myths, and playtime form part of the pedagogical devices by which this is instilled such that when we read aloud, 'And the bear said, "Who's been sleeping in my bed,"' it is a multifaceted narrative moment for asking the child to imagine occupying another's space and emotions. In this case, the language and the activity of recitation train their minds to perform such projections which locks in with their daily routines of 'play' acting, whereby toys train their minds how to impersonate adult behaviors and impersonate inanimate objects like plastic trains and dolls.

Cartoons do the same thing with non-humanoid projections like wily mice and dumb cats, robots, and talking trees. Handling small objects daily teaches fundamental storytelling skills, skills that are far more complex than monkey-see-and-do.

***

When Professor Gaster drew the triangle, was he impersonating it somehow? Did he literally draw me in as well?

Notwithstanding, we are helped in this process by our muscular-skeletal system. Even if we lacked a pedagogic culture of imagining what others feel, our bodies would take care of the job anyway. This is because we occupy space and become sounding boards for assessing how deep that space is through movement and tactile sensations. Tentative motion, even with a handicap such as audial or visual impairment, reduces the breadth of familiarity with one's physical depth of field. With a cane, for instance, you'll cautiously tap from each individual step to another discharging small segments of progress with a distinctly proscribed sensation for traversing distance. What this does is embed you in the moment between two steps rather than embed you in a transit motion in which the steps are elided.

Compare this to the more fluid act of riding a horse over hills with the wind at your back. It's like drawing a line with a single, long stroke versus constructing one by tiny connective dots. You can see this difference best with Adobe programs such as Photoshop versus Illustrator. You can use a 'paint brush' to mimic your movement, which delivers a line as a unique swipe, or you can go to Illustrator and using the pen tool, methodically tap, tap, tap, point to point - to construct a line like a blind person.

All that's really different are the increments of motion. Yet it is a world of cognitive difference. It's stating the obvious that the degrees of change in anything are always significant and that we manage our lives accordingly. When the increments of motion are smaller as they are small for those who are blind, the tendency is to live in a flatter world in which spatial depth is very much limited to the aggregation of sequential steps, one after the other. Therefore, each point along the way begs for more heightened awareness and attention, constraining you to the incremental process of being 'between' far more than to the summary affect. You can't see the forest for the trees.

It sounds counterintuitive that blind people's super tactile sensitivity, which is far more alert to three-dimensional form than others, nevertheless confines them to a flatter world. But remember, it is the content in the cranial mechanism that directs how we 'think' about the world. Removing the obvious navigational tool that is 'sight' is removing the visual goal and the world of anticipation, the part that ties up the small increments of motion into a summary activity toward a unique reward. It limits the facility of steering the body as an object through space and makes the process feel more shallow.

The blinded British theologian John Hull explains this sense of bondage to highly restrictive motion as limiting one's horizon to the perimeter of skin.

> I think that for a blind person there is no intermediate space. Things are either there or they're not there.

There is no sense of transitional degrees, no overview of coming or going. And therefore, as he suggests, no sense of 'almost' there. Without a goal of distant space, there is no intermediate space bounded by both a physical process and intellectual anticipation. But if you can't see your goal and can't look back to see how far you have come, then every motion is essentially intermediate, and wherever you are *is* absolutely intermediate space.

***

Therefore, sight extends our ability to comprehend our own three dimensionality by playing off an active versus passive duality. Whereas other senses are passive and specific to a single organ. You receive rather than project smell through your nose, taste through your tongue, sound through your ears, rather than projecting it through them. Vision is altogether different.

True, your eyes don't project images like a film projector. Rather, they seem to perform a passive function (i.e., receive photons, the interpretation of which is an active mental response). But the difference that explains the need for far more cortical real estate than the other senses require is that when I see the world, the implicit reciprocity is that I am also aware of it seeing me back.

It is not a ridiculous leap of faith to believe that if I can constantly see myself performing in every frame of my existence, others can see me too. All of which reinforces this notion of 'self' as an object contained in existence. The notion of 'anticipation' is lacking for every other sensation, yet always present for vision. If a musical note is sounded beyond a schema with which you are already familiar, there is no element of anticipating more, nor when or how.

***

One of my favorite stories about my mother is utterly graphic and dependent on the dramatic effect of deep space with regard to this duality. As a little girl she was allowed to meet her glamorous mother debark the Queen Elizabeth ocean liner after an Atlantic crossing. Abroad for weeks, my mother couldn't wait to greet her. Separated by Customs and fences and crowds, it was easy to pick out the shape of her mother's distinct and enormous hat growing larger and larger as she emerged out of deep space to embrace her child.

My mother was in effect the vicarious agent of her own mother's response, as much as her own. Her vision allowed her to intuit when and how her mother would see this precious object, her own self, just as her mother was doing the same. The anticipation and reward were so much sweeter because of the vast horizon against which she tracked her mother's approach toward her.

In fact, for four-year-old's, vision is in the far field horizon and they are not yet able to sweep their gaze laterally. Later, they generally become myopic, more focused on objects close at hand and less conversant with depth. This is probably because they no longer require it for learning about self and other; that has already been accomplished and is part of their mechanical brain. Why this happens to be the case is curious and perhaps significant for the training we require during early childhood to appreciate the fact, albeit not the words of John Donne: 'No man is an island entire of itself; every man is a piece of the continent, a part of the main.'

Our life history seems to train us for a variety of visual expectations, as if to equip us for the community glue that is any 'Theory of Mind' and the ability to anticipate behavior in others based on oneself. But John Hull reminds us that sound can give a sort of, 'Horizon of place within which you can situate yourself.' It is not vicarious because you cannot anticipate sound, it happens to you and around you. Nevertheless, it is a kind of enslavement to sequential coordinates on a graph that mark the intersection of only two inputs, motion/touch with sound.

Plot the points and you have your frame of reference, your axis of reality, which is why Oliver Sacks referred to this in *An Anthropologist on Mars*:

> We, with a full complement of senses, live in space and time; the blind live in a world of time alone…Indeed, if we can no longer see in space, then the idea of space becomes incomprehensible…. (p. 124)

I'm unsure whether I would commit 100% to this notion of complete spatial deficit because I am not sure how to express visual depth on its purest level (see subsequent chapters.) I don't think anyone is. But we can try to work toward an understanding of perceived depth from the bottom up, quite literally from the soles of the feet and palms of the hand to our central control box brain.

***

We start with minute receptors lodged in our limbs to give us information about our position as an object in space, regardless of vision. Chip Wood, a long-time educator, has spent decades observing childhood development. In his handbook for teachers and parents, *Yard Sticks*, he explains how kindergarten learning is achieved best:

> This is an age where much learning is transmitted through the large muscles. Learning goes from hand to head, not the other way around. (Wood 1992:33)

Even as adults, we continue this process, as Robertson Davies says in his 1985 novel '*What's Bred in the Bone*', '…the hand speaks to the brain as surely as the brain speaks to the hand.' But this is also true of our larger limbs. When that same jogger approaches head on, your body 'feels' the presence of this motion into your space and adjusts immediately. I would suggest that if you are particularly keen to focusing on one extremity, you might think you feel a kind of sharp or irritated feeling as the movement of your body and the jogger bounce vibrations in tighter wavelengths until you finally pass each other. Our very own Doppler effect.

Think of the sound of an approaching train and how the noise increases to a peak, falling off much faster when it passes than it did as it approached. This is the classic Doppler effect where the approaching sound waves increasingly compress around you whereas they fall off if you are behind the motion due to a lack of build-up. Your body can sense the same things if you just listen to your skin 'crawl.'

This could also be an effect of anticipation coupled with emotions such as irritation and annoyance. Regardless of how or why, we all sense impending pressure on our personal space and make immediate adjustments. That sensation is real.

***

You'd certainly remark that vision plays a tremendous role in this sensitivity toward approaching and therefore encroaching objects, which it obviously does, and largely by way of the vestibular or balance apparatus. This is a mini system lodged in your inner ear, accurately called the labyrinth because of its many interconnected channels. This five-part apparatus adjusts for balance by steering your head like a rudder in a turbulent sea. It stabilizes your gaze so you can maintain focus during motion.

But it also sensitizes you to your physical orientation in space apart from vision by auto-correcting your position, which in the extreme is how we break our fall - not by countering with the opposite limb, but by tensing the affected limb. Recall that when you lose your footing with, say, your left leg, you try to bear the weight by skipping it out ahead of the other foot.

I'm no neurobiologist nor audiologist, so I'll just introduce some of what is going on. For example, monitoring these infinite varieties of head pitches and rolls resides in the 'otolith' organs called 'utricle' and 'saccule,' which sound like some Scandinavian myth about twin trolls. Comprised of three semicircular canals, the hair or nerve cells lining these structures in very specific patterns are predisposed to detect only one kind of movement: yaw, roll, or pitch.

Yaw is when I shake my head from side to side as we do when emphasizing 'no.' Pitch is the up and down move, working against gravitational pull, that we all employ for a hearty 'yes.' And roll is a head tilt, best described if you imagine a child with an ear infection trying to assuage the pain by touching ear to shoulder. All of these nerve fibers signal the brain to adjust body and gaze to maintain overall balance and posture.

But there's a problem. The brain elicits motion orders slower than the movements themselves. If we see, say, a ball coming our way, by the time the brain has processed this and sent a message to move the hand, the ball would be in a different place and we'd miss it every time. What makes it all work is how we learn to anticipate placement and motion such that we predict it all out on a mental grid and model about linking these disparate timeframes. If we didn't anticipate where our motions should ultimately take us, the slower-acting brain at two hundred milliseconds behind motion would throw off all the calculations and have us extend a hand to catch a ball that already zipped by. Living would be dizzy, un-focused, and virtually useless.

We'd be useless.

Here's how to think about it: Hunters shoot an arrow at a target that is always considerably ahead of the moving animal to compensate for the speed of its running. Think of that arrow as our brain, which simultaneously assesses two points, both one's present physical position and the target position, and then calculates.

Another example is how a ballerina uses this same predictive compensation. When she preps for a pirouette, she fixes her eyes *only* on a landing point, and with the intention of keeping her head as steadfastly pinned to it as long as possible and her head as close to 360 degrees as possible. She knows that the momentum of her spin will exceed her cognitive ability to digest multiple phases of the spin and confuse her balancing messages from the cerebellum along the way. She decides, yes decides, to override it and fixate on the future position of her landing.

***

Dizziness is an aspect of mentally living seconds behind in the past and adjusting too slowly to ramped up movement. Studies have shown that dancers acquire the habit of hijacking the cortical feed of the cerebellum, where most motion directives are processed to the neocortex. An extreme and intentional compensation of the lag motion in the eye for focus counterbalances the faster movement of the body. But it is merely an aspect of the means by which we proprio-perceive (i.e., self-perceive as a three-dimensional object in space) by collecting data about ourselves contextually and with the complete confidence of continuity.

**

Now back to our jogger in the path of oncoming runners. Although the final directive to hurry up and move one inch to the left to avoid a head-on collision might have been issued from your brain, the leg or forearm or torso is picking up vibrations that sense space and motion first. Our physical positioning is determined by the tensing and release of joints, of holding and adjusting them, which is somewhat of a macro version of grasping objects in your hand.

Both are directed largely through sensitive calculations which are communicated to your brain by muscle spindles. Contained within them are two kinds of fibers that work in tandem to plot your limb dynamics. One reads the velocity and direction of motion, and the other ascertains position. As far as we know, that is.

We do not absorb objects from without; they are as much abstractions as is any triangle. We merely transfer code from these various sensing devices in our epidermis and joints. And unsurprisingly, there are far more devices in far greater numbers imbedded in our far more limber finger tips.

A few numbers to chew on: For the joint spindles alone, you have to calculate that there are nine joints per hand, nine interphalangeal joints that articulate five fingers in comparison to a solitary knee joint in the leg. Obviously, the density of these receptors called proprio-ceptors (receptors for self) vary.

> Large muscles that generate coarse movements have relatively few spindles, in contrast extra-ocular muscles and the intrinsic muscles of the hand and neck are richly supplied with spindles, reflecting the importance of accurate eye movements, the need to manipulate objects with great finesse and continuous demand for precise positioning of the head. (Purves et al 2012:217)

We have in our hands a variety of sensors to deal with the outside world. We have the ones mentioned above that remit information to the brain about the positioning of our joints and are exclusively tuned to our unique physical self. They're happy if I just claw the air or stretch my fingers. But there are others that key into stimuli from other sources such as a pin prick, which is hardly a singular but rather a crisp cluster of sensations. First there's the feel of the metal, the size of the tip, then the pressure, then the pain. The inputs are an interplay and constant tradeoff between agility and sensation.

But orchestrating our fingers didn't happen overnight. Grasping objects is not unique to our species. We aren't the only primate with opposable thumbs, but we are the only one that manages to sweep the ring and small finger across our palm to reach it, where our cousins only manage as far as the index finger. Called the ulnar opposition, it allowed us to cup our hands and develop fine motor skills that required evolution of special sensors called mechano-receptors.

I love that term because it implies the mechanical system in place for operating these miniature cranes of ours. I remember as a child, the vending machine that had a sealed glass box containing wonderful little stuffed animals and an annoying toy crane (we still have these, but the toys are much larger). We couldn't touch the darn toys directly, much like our own sealed-off cortex. Instead, we had to conduct the claw or bucket on the crane remotely with levers by opening and closing it at the right juncture to pick up a toy and drop it down the chute. Luckily, we had already developed a fine sense of space and texture to make the right adjustments remotely.

We knew the behavior of plush toys, what we didn't know was the behavior of this annoying crane because we couldn't sympathize with what it sensed. We couldn't at first 'sensualize' it, which is why I rarely, if ever, won. I never won. If only some information about how the claws felt could have been conducted back, maybe I'd have known better how to win the prize. More nickels and quarters would have helped as my fingers began to learn its mechanical ways better, as my fingers could become psychological extensions of the crane itself.

***

Here's Chip Walters in his book '*Thumbs, Toes and Tears*':

> The physical power and dexterity of our thumbs and
> hands make them central to humanity. Their

biological evolution literally changed our minds. They
enabled us to better manipulate the world around us
and the manipulation of things then came to also
mold our minds....

This evolutionary concept lying somewhere between Darwinian nature versus Humanists' nurture theories at this point can neither be condemned nor celebrated, which is fine with me. As an artist, if I must reduce civilization to a unique development, you'd think it would be Walter's version. It has problems though when figuring out why the Neanderthals, who also had the ulnar opposition, didn't leave much trace records of their having put it to particularly good use.

That is, except for the Bruniquel cave in southwestern, France. Breached by spelunkers in 1990 for the first time, a thousand meters beyond the entrance were found curious constructions of rough semi circles made of stalagmite chunks of equal sizes and dating back over 150,000 years and possibly twenty thousand years earlier than that. Other than this unique artifact attributed to Neanderthals, they have not been known to have demonstrated much architectural or design innovations. Perhaps they lacked the variety and degree of manual receptors. Perhaps not, because then you have to try to work into this model the fact that it took our Cro-Magnon ancestors nearly 150,000 years to start making excellent use of theirs.

Or perhaps both species just worked their human magic in organic materials until they discovered how to work the same magic in stone and sediments. This makes far greater sense. But there's one more possibility to add to the mix. The genius, the evolutionary and random genetic 'sport' that discovers things no one else had, and the enormous leaps made by others integrating and building on them.

At any rate, the whole 'artifying' riff, co-terminus with the origin of our species, is extremely poetic, and I'll keep this one simmering on the back burner.

***

Until now, we've left out the 'Coordinator Maximus,' the brain as the willful churner of data, a process commonly called 'cognition,' the overused buzzword of the day. That's why some scientists at the turn of the millennium compared it to the Universe as the greatest self-organizing system around, almost as an act of exasperation. Or maybe desperation. We were learning more and more at a geometric speed about our brains, and as with most accelerated discoveries, finding more and more we couldn't fathom about the way all the parts worked together.

It is tempting to seek cover from 'cognition' debates in philosophy because the behavior of 'knowing' is a slippery slope. But it always comes back to the brain's iconic preference for organizing itself. You might not like that your mind edited your sweet reveries about the moon over the Seine by cutting to a red rubber ball that you lost ten years ago, but you are a captive audience. The decision was probably made a long time ago; it was just waiting for the right cue.

Thankfully, proprioception allows us, for the purpose of this discussion, to work from the bottom up and leave top-down conundrums to the sages. It allows us to work from personal and empirical data versus theory, which is really why I undertook writing this book, to give scientists a bit of a worm's eye view of what motivates us 'image makers.' Knowing 'about' objects also has a lot to do with personal history, acquired habit, and remembered patterns of behavior. The fact is that no two people see the same thing the same way, and if you don't believe me, then I'll let Heinrich Wöfflin set this up with his opening paragraph from '*Kunstgeschichtliche Grundbegriffe*,' his 1915 book on the 'Principles of Art History':

> Ludwig Richter relates in his reminiscences how once
> when he was in Tivoli as a young man, he and three
> friends set out to paint part of the landscape, all four
> firmly resolved not to deviate from nature by a hair's
> breadth; and although the subject was the same and each
> quite creditably reproduced what his eyes had seen, the
> result was four totally different pictures, as different from
> each other as the personalities of the four painters.

This served as Wöfflin's introduction on 'style,' but it also leads nicely to the idiosyncratic process of 'knowing' so reasonably expounded some three hundred fifty years ago by the Scotsman David Hume. There is a certain amount of common sense to his philosophy (i.e., the observation that habitual behavior enforces belief in its behavioral constancy). The brain then lays this in as a deep track that routes both our anticipation and response to future such events, however small. He called this a 'necessary connection' between cause and effect, the result of a fairly instinctive calculating or determination that after an undisclosed number of exposures to some one thing or typical thing, you can project what it ought to do in the future.

History has given him a bit of a hard time, but neuroscience has proven to be a friend. We now know that each brain physically strengthens its 'habit' of anticipating objects by sprouting new synaptic branches of its dendrites, the bushy part of the nerve connectors certifying that behavior necessarily be recalled. But it also suppresses the chemical ability of other dendrites so the routine doesn't get too muddled and dispersed. This is called 'synaptic suppression,' and it's a very helpful thing.

Of course, I am greatly simplifying all to make the point: Shapes are not simple things on blackboards. They depend on our ability to grasp objects and the information we routinely generate from the physical activity. This comes by way of not necessarily grabbing hold of triangles, which I have never done. I have drawn them. But also of anticipating the nature of certain lines by virtue of having assimilated the full-bodied experience previously and often.

***

Our bodies are overly informed with conflicting and ambiguous stimuli such that everything we do is a suppression of potential actions for a more relevant one to dominate and thereby become what we call 'choice.' When I sit at my table to cut out a shape, I have somehow whipped through all the permutations of possibilities for a three-edged contour, suppressed them and focused on one. If you were looking at me while I did this, you'd notice a kind of blank stare as I focused inward to 'see' this shape. I have often felt it easier to fix an image in my mind when my eyes are slightly tilted to the right and have wondered if this weren't some outward indication of an internal neuro positioning device. But regardless, this is not just a mental game. My fingers have told me first what the criteria are for making this selection, and that lesson was learned in infancy.

Fibers in my fingers relate all matter of touch sensitivity data, including pressure, texture, and size, back to my brain. They conduct this somatic (motor) sensory information toward it (in Latin, *ad*) rather than away from it (*ex* or efferent) because they collect rather than decide, and are thus called afferent fibers, the root meanings: to carry toward. Housed in my fingers tips, they coil up tightly into (so far as we know) four types of mechanoreceptors that have varying responsibilities.

For example, when I touch a cat's fur, I am not assessing size and shape, but rather nuanced motion and vibration against my skin. I have 'rapidly adapting afferents' that immediately spring to attention at the onset of stimuli but calm down when they have established a pattern of stimulation such as a texture. This makes a lot of sense to me and is consistent with the brain's typical behavior of habituating to non-alarming sensations by establishing routines, in this case, minute but regularized sensations from individual hairs in a cluster. Fur is a cluster of enormous quantities of hair.

Imagine how nerve-racking it would be to identify the sensation of each single hair. Your day would be as confined to infinitely 'living through' each unique sensation and you'd get nothing done. The first human would never have gotten past 'start.'

Most mechanoreceptors in the hand, or dermis for that matter, are rapid adapters that sense onset of pressure, then dumb themselves down until the pressure is suddenly altered as from lessening or removing the stimulus. That's the Ying of sensory adaptation. They are very welcome when it comes to sensing vibrations and speed. Otherwise we'd be trapped in constant and minute fluctuations.

What's the Yang?

Differentiating and isolating are essential cognitive activities for archiving knowledge and therefore survival. Also of art. Art is but another tool we felt compelled to invent to add to our arsenal of tools, specifically to expedite these two activities: differentiating and isolating. Please understand this.

Let's have a little fun and say that you just lost a diamond among a pile of equally sized pebbles. Maybe the light is low and so it doesn't really help to guide you in this panicky search. The fast adapting sensors in your fingers have acclimated to the overall sensation of equal-sized stones and basically taken a long lunch break as you continue to pass your fingers across all the pebbles. No new news there. What you need is something sensitive enough to probe the differences of hardness, shape, edge, and form, those subtle qualities that describe the diamond rather than the pebble.

The harder you seek, the more fascinating becomes the behavior of your hand. First you use your palm, then as the search intensifies, you rake with the under surface of your long fingers until only your second and third fingers are extended. Not the thumb. What you are doing is calling on the fingers that are most compacted with 'slowly adapting afferents.' These are the mechanoreceptors that cannot diffuse and pause their feedback, but rather treat stimuli as separate events. Slower is more sensitive. Rushed is cursory and sloppy. What child isn't taught that same thing?

When the 'two-point threshold' is applied to test for simultaneous sensitivity of two stimuli of distances 3.5mm to 2mm, or even fewer, only the tips of your fingers lead the way. These are the Merkel receptors feeding back data in bytes from stimuli that interpret a neural picture of size and shape, and are thankfully especially sensitive to edges and points, like cut diamonds.

But wait - look at the positioning of your hand now. The palm, with a receptive field of two-point sensitivity of 9mm, is useless. So is the base of your finger, with a receptive field of about 6mm. Still can't find the diamond? You lower your head and finally extend the smartest of all the fingers, in fact, the smartest sensory probe we have, because it contains the slower neural messengers in the very greatest density. Everyone instinctively knows it's not the opposable thumb.

When you want to feel the newly sharpened edge of a knife you use the thumb. It's a bit more robust against fine sharpness and not as squeamish. Most tend to answer that the thumb is the 'smart' finger because the surface area is larger and we have come to trust its opposable anchoring function. Except that were I to ask you to draw your initials in the air, you would stick out your index finger.

This is not a coincidence because the 'pointer finger' is indeed our most discriminating tool finger. In fact, it is our body's most alert tactile radar, and well beyond other parts of the hand. And way beyond that of our upper lip, cheek, toes, and nose, which is rather surprising. You'd at least think it were the lips and mouth area as it is with a dog. The homunculus, or the diagramming of our somatosensory cortex according to the neural areas specific to body parts, indicates the hand and mouth as the areas most sensitive to stimulation.

But most of these diagrams fail to drill down on the hand components themselves. Therefore, despite what anthropologists emphasize about our unique thumb, I'd stress the index finger and then go find a deep hole to stick my head in since I'm no biologist. But it's true. I would even make a bold bet that the deficit of afferent receptors per square inch in the index finger of the chimp or gorilla in comparison to us is greater than it is for the thumb. In other words, there is a bigger difference in the number of receptors between the ape and human index finger than there is for the thumb. Just a thought, and hoping some anthropologist takes the measurements.

But you don't need science to demonstrate the comparable acuity of this particular digit over others when you see it at work from infancy. A baby will demonstrate this by the age of six months when parents introduce it to the charming book '*Pat the Bunny.*' They will tuck in their other fingers, (yes, the thumb!) and extend out their second finger. Through this process, they can best explore and probe new touch and shape sensations and come to know about the difference between their mother's smooth chin and the rapid onslaught of new tactile sensations from the 'bunny' book like polyester, fake fur, vinyl, etc.

Probing is a good word that describes why we use the index finger. It is by virtue of biological attributes that we feel more confident determining space, volume, and texture this way. The thumb is trumped by the tip of the index finger for the proliferation of Merkel receptors. And as has often been demonstrated by Paul Bach y Rita, Norman Doige, and so many others, the somatosensory cortex is somewhat plastic and can reorganize itself to a degree as can other parts of the brain, but within boundaries. Thus, the homunculus diagram changes according to our body status. Cut off the tips of my fingers and after a while, that diagram of enormous hands is sure to recede.

***

Let's talk a little more about these incredible tactile sensors and how they color memories and theories of mind like understanding so well what a professor might feel as he drags a rigid piece of chalk across black slate.

While parents call out the name to go with the feeling in *Pat the Bunny*, the little fingers have decided to ramp up these rapidly adapting afferents in the face of ongoing stimulation, while the slowly adapting ones take a back seat. After all, this is a book about texture not objects. This crowding out effect seems to be because our fingers just have too many information collectors available that would jam the system were they all working simultaneously at a fever pitch. Honestly, nothing we do ever employs more than one train of emphatic data processing over others. Others might be available, but they are not tuned up unless we shift the focus.

But wait. The index finger is still extended. For the child, these textures are part of a new form. There is an isolation and probing discovery to be made here, a cataloging of something new.

***

We're not entirely sure about every sensor in our fingers but it scopes out like this: there are four mechanoreceptors in the three layers of our skin. By far, the greater work horses seem to inhabit our epidermis and just a bit lower in our dermis. Exclusively populating our epidermis are the Merkel cells, which account for nearly 25% of all the receptors in our hand.

Residing in the nadir of ridges responsible for finger prints, these receptors can define spatial resolution to the highest degree. In this case, our index finger tip can discern detail of 0.5mm, which is 1.89 pixels. Think of your printing program again, that a resolution of 300 per standard square inch is awfully decent. This means that in one square inch you have three hundred rows and three hundred columns of these little things. The resolution of sensation in your finger is a bit better than 150 per square inch. That is still twice as much that is needed for graphics on the web!

Compare this to other fingers whose point acumen lags far behind, with a clumsy target of 2mm in diameter. And to drive this point further, consider applying the dual tips of a tweezer to your forearm. You will not perceive the difference between the points until they are spread out to 40 millimeters and even more for your back. Ergo the tale of the 'Princess and the Pea,' whose back was as sensitive as her fingers, a pea measuring on average around 2 millimeters. They had to invent a tale conflating royalty with heightened perception to explain the rarity. It was a nice touch.

Merkel cells are sensitive to points and contours like the sharp tip of a needle and are excellent for tracking form. They are our first line of defense against injury, almost twice as dense are our Meissner corpuscles. Populating the dermis just below the ridges of our skin, they are four times as sensitive to skin abrasion (i.e., deformation). And curiously, very curiously, they depopulate by a factor of four from the age of fifteen to fifty, which says a lot about life histories and our diminishing need to probe new things and truly 'know about things' as we get older.

Further, they are reactive to the lowest level of vibrations at 5Hz to 15Hz, or revolutions per second, in comparison to the fastest mechanoreceptor called Pacinian, which can detect vibrations as high as 300 Hz and whose solitary function is just that, to detect vibrations. These rapidly adapting receptors are called phasic because they detect the onslaught of vibrations but do not sustain their sensitivity throughout the event until, and only until the event ceases.

***

When I walk across the Brooklyn Bridge, I sometimes concentrate on hearing and feeling my feet hit the wood. If I do, I can't see the famous vista of water sweeping out beneath me. I'd be lying if I said I did. But when I take my walking for granted, I am shifting back to an implicit behavioral function that I acquired as a matter of course and can now see the tug coming under the bridge, and what a tremendous sight! Nevertheless, this is a distinct decision I have made. I cannot concentrate on both simultaneously. The brain likes to tell one story at a time, even if they are lightning fast and efficient little narratives.

For the infant, is it more urgent to feel the fur of the bunny or hold the object? Recent studies by Scott Johnson of UCLA deposed the old Piaget predilection for some innate grasping reflex and suggest that we acquire the mechanics through observation; that indeed, this ability is not born into us. In other words, there is no grasping gene. But I still need to be convinced. No matter what, even at three months of age we are busy sorting, filing, and figuring. Our brain wants to color up one flow of data above the other at any given moment.

The same holds true when creating objects. You actually are *re*creating by shunting back and forth between the afferent inputs as well. You are switching back and forth between your implicit memory of texture and shape, information that you have processed since birth. As you begin to formulate an image, you enter into the idea by means of one particular sensation stream over another. Is assessing volume and size of greater import, or is it texture, temperature, and other such values?

Let's say I am folding a piece of paper down the middle. Am I more concerned about size than texture? Are my fingers sending back information about the edges and therefore dimensions, or about the roughness of the surface? If I am trying to answer questions of size, edge, and volume, my slowly adapting afferents shout down my rapidly firing ones. For example, my Merkel receptors closest to the outer layer of my skin connect to fibers that are more effective at channeling information to my spinal cord and up to my brain when there is less obstruction and ambiguity. They want to predominate.

How is this decision made? Ah, there's the rub, we just don't quite know. But here's a bit of a riddle. Due to the speed of synaptic connections, we seem to decide what we're going to do before the message is consciously 'known' in our more sophisticated frontal cortex. I have already determined that the rock I want to draw intrigues me first for its texture before its shape. I can 'feel it' on my hand. We all do, but don't realize it until called on to isolate the thought stream as artists must do constantly. I wish I had a functional MRI locked on my head to prove that the Pacinian receptors are firing faster and not only because they predominate at 800 in the palm of my hand (350 per finger) but because of what they are good at detecting. Luckily, Kenneth O Johnson, who passed away far too young, devoted himself to just this.

> Combined psychophysical and neurophysiological experiments show that an important consequence of this function is the perception of distant events through transmitted vibrations when we grasp an object in the hand. When we become skilled in the use of a probe or a tool, we perceive events at the working surface of the tool or probe as though our fingers were present. *The PC afferents are responsible for this critical perceptual capacity.* (My italics.) (Johnson:458)

They are brilliant for detecting distal objects.

Long before Johnson came along, humans knew this. On a more macro level, there is a reason that the soles of our feet and palms of our hands for us and all primates are hairless, or glabrous. We need an unobstructed sounding board like water is to radar and air is for light waves to pick up the signals needed for us to ascertain the attributes of objects for the purpose of manipulation. This is called stereognosis.

Figuring out your relative body position in space, as already mentioned, is called proprioception, relative to distal objects, that is. Knowing about yourself as an object is a lifesaving evaluation (some call it a reflex) that allows me to risk squeezing between two cars at a red light and knowing I'll get through. I understand my volume in a comparative context. All of us do this when eying racks of clothes. We know just by looking at a pair of pants what will and what won't fit. Some of us are more in touch with their personal volumes than others.

These are rapid decisions made that involve replacements of our body icon with something or someone similar in our mind's eye. In this case the imagined self in the outfit. Once again, the anterior cingulate cortex reenters the game. Some say I am taking the well-documented pain empathy paradigm that is condign for this neuron cluster much too far. But I'm not. Consider why.

This is the well-documented effect of empathizing with another's pain or poor decision-making, meaning that their error will cause a bad outcome with which each of us can identify, unless that pro-social is determined to be worthless and abhorrent. So, there is a judgment factor at work here, a high-order cognitive and diffuse assessment of why a given target for the ACC (Anterior Cingulate Cortex) is valid or not.

> The ACC receives inputs from these structures (limbic and insulae) relative to the differences between expected and actual outcomes of a given decision and provides outputs to coordinate dorsolateral prefrontal structures in order to organize behavioral responses. (Lavin et al.:2013/7/64)

I dare say that the more agile you are and the more you flex your limbs, the more detailed are the coordinates your brain has to ascertain your three-dimensionality relative to the outside world. And the high frequency vibration receptors just discussed like the Pacinian corpuscles predominate in that agility in these joint and muscle spindles. This is why I really do move away from an oncoming jogger because I really do 'feel' the compression of their vibrations as they approach. And it all translates as being an emotional reaction. It is very, very annoying. I get angry.

**

There is nothing in human existence that better illustrates this remarkable sensibility to one's own personal volume than our stone age forbears. They knew they could pass through dark cave holes and chambers without much light, if any at all. We know they had very few proprio-sensate mishaps because no skeletons have been found in these chutes and passages. I have been in a few of these recesses myself, most recently in the hills surrounding Rhonda in Andalusia, Spain.

Off the main chamber are vertiginous drops, trenches, and tunnels, replete with paintings done twenty thousand years ago. I never ventured into those. But the thought that someone did and that on the first round did so without knowing whether they could get out or what was at the other end was remarkable enough. Just think of the risk, the daring, perhaps even their tender relationship with cold, jagged, unforgiving bedrock. Maybe they had a pet dog sniff and lead the way. I would have.

But most importantly, think of their comfort level when shimmying through these small spaces such that they could envision it as a canvas and execute the task. It says so much about their mental construct of themselves as a relative object in a small encased volume, and that they understood their personal dimensions far better than most of us today.

Honestly, I never would have tried it. But my son would have snaked through an unknown passage in a heartbeat. As a boxer, his muscle spindles and vestibular system have tuned his brain so well to his autobiographical dimension that it would be an instantaneous act for him to evaluate if he could fit. I, on the other hand, was confused, and out of my element. Scared. Anxious. Sadly, my sedentary life had dulled the feedback from my limbs. I didn't trust their ability to measure all the parts of me.

**

This innate calculating is also a lifesaver that allows hatchlings, for example, to duck in their nests when the shadow of a hawk flies over, or for a young Vervet monkey to run for the bush. Much work is being done on these inherited survival codes or endogenous memories. It is very difficult to distinguish evolutionary instinct from hereditary or acquired routine. Again, there is nothing truly definitive to report. However, Niko Tinbergen isolated, to an extent, particular shape alarms for avian hatchlings just having burst through their shells. People quote him often, but you can use any animal biologist's findings to corroborate the same species-specific, symbolic identifications.

He maintains that silhouettes of birds with short necks moving in a specific and relative direction trigger crouching for some nestlings. It depends on an overall sense of one's size in a small space (i.e., a nest).

Certainly, this is very intriguing in isolation, and momentous if it has universal implications. Continuing with this notion of innate cognizance of one's body as an object, the young Vervet monkey learns sound alarms and appropriate survival responses by observing and then mimicking the mother. She instantaneously seeks cover in a tree to avoid a hungry leopard, and her loud bark is her warning to her young to do the same. More than just the sounds emitted, there has to be a keen sense of one's body in terms of maximizing the best route and shortest distance to attain safety. How is this done?

***

I know about shapes because I have seen them, constructed them, lifted them, felt around them, walked on them, crashed into them, avoided them, climbed them, swallowed them, held them, and ascertained their characteristic textures. I have their routines etched into my brain.

Some scientists have good reason to believe that if one aspect of your sensory system teeters and stumbles, your relative interpretative acumen lags the norm. For example, recent research on the vestibular module for learning-disabled children suggests that deficits in the inner ear degrade their ability to draw. Although this plugs in nicely with our discussion, I include it with a cautionary note that far more studies need to be conducted. It might have more to do with general creativity rather than balance and hand/eye coordination. So, we have to be really careful here, intriguing as it is.

Nevertheless, based on purely anecdotal commentary, namely my own, I must restate the obvious that drawing facility fades the less you do it. In art-speak, we call it getting rusty. You see the shape better the more you draw it, and you can't draw it unless you grasp a tool or point your fingers, the index finger is best, in a very determined miming event.

Physically tracing the shape transduces it as a mental tracing by way of an impossibly enormous number of individual bytes of data that the brain then captures as a collected identity. But remember, to you it is a fluid act when in fact it is also an impossibly large number of tiny data points best illustrated by non-vector graphics. When you draw a line in high resolution and blow it up, you can see the string of tiny pixels that define it. This is miniscule in comparison to the information you are really shunting back to the 'Great Decider.'

And once again, how is this done? The answer: We don't know. We don't know why some data points are more defining and impactful than others, why we decided that, on what basis, and how we felt when doing so. We don't know how and where we store these, the application or plan by which we collect them, where we store that blueprint, and whether it is innate.

The bottom line is that the more you draw, the better you draw. This must be important to the condition of recognition. Execution and practice makes the icon you store more precise and ironically more catholic and elastic in its matching up of multiple versions. If I draw a head more often than you, I assure you I will spot it faster in camouflage.

Every act of drawing is an act of living the object through proprio-sensation. We'll see more of this in the next chapter called 'Tracks of My Fears.'

What we are really addressing is a notion of fluency. Mimicry of perceived objects with the hand directly stimulates our cognitive dictionary. And most essential during image-making is whether one can stereotype: How much do we know 'about' it? This is a very self-conscious cognitive process right up there with 'What shall I wear today?' When you create an image, be it a pattern or object, you are processing a continuous string of questions and answers. You ask yourself, 'How much do I know about what a hand looks like?' It is curiously as much a negative exercise as a positive one. When I draw, I am always wondering how far I can deviate from each basket of attributes before I lose an effect; how far down can I edit this scene without losing its impact?

This is a question and game with which all artists and image-makers trifle. It is both a titillation of perceived reality and a constant intellectual struggle of distilling phenomena. If we 'know about' an object, then at what point do we go too far such that it is no longer pertinent to its specific category?

This is beginning to sound a lot like a true language with a precise vocabulary despite what so many anthropologists believe; that true image-making depends on symbolism *first as a verbal construct*. In other words, verbal language keys everything into our brains. 'Art' is *a posteriori* to the words we have already invented for the objects.

In art, it's not just a question of grouping associations as it can be in verbal constructs; the fixed and internal relationship of qualities within the set defines the object so that if you scramble the hierarchy of linkage or skew the syntax, you have scrambled the picture and therefore the meaning.

Here's a really fun question to chew on: Just as there is Wernicke's Area in the rostral or rear of the Sylvian Fissure or lateral sulcus (usually only left lobe, but not in a consistently specific location) that can combine sounds to make words but cannot ascribe meaning or symbolism, where is that pictorial mate in the brain? Where is the part of the brain that can assemble lines and shapes syntactically to draw standard forms while the protagonist hasn't got a clue what it is? Where is that iconographic parallel to Wernicke's aphasia or fluency aphasia as the verbal agnosia is called? If Broca's Area or Brodmann 44 and 45 seem to be requisite for connecting meaning to sounds, does Broca's Area do the same for shapes?

It would not be overstating the case that most point to the development of the left lobe of the brain as the linguistic side in most of us, which has shown consistently to be of greater volume than the right. Just move your finger behind your left ear and feel the bump there in comparison to the right ear. There is a kind of cortical asymmetry called the Yakovlevian Torque. For example, the frontal lobe on the right protrudes farther forward, and in some like Einstein, bulges to the side. Whereas, the Sylvian fissure or crease between the temporal and frontal lobes is generally longer on the left side, suggesting more cortical area and sometimes up to ten times the size of the right. This area houses most identifiable areas specific to language and 'meaning' functionality.

I certainly hope that theorists aren't basing their ideas regarding the evolution of human civilization on this or a rather myopic predilection for ranking verbal language over visual! If that were the case, we would not now need to be inserting a whole menu of emoticons or repurposed grammatical symbols like colons and parentheses into our texts to curtail the ambiguity of written language.

To be fair, the right side generally ascribed to the visual weighs more and develops first and faster in newborns. And the Yakovlevian Torque exists for all mammals and then some. So, is the complement of Brodmann 44 larger on the right and does it code for shape understanding just as it codes for language meaning on the left?

Essential to visual linguistics is this dialogue, at what degree of tilting away, say, for those two convergent lines on the black board, do they lose their suggestion of things to come? At what point is their 'V' shape no longer implicit? Obviously, there is some distinct point of no return; a moment, an angle at which they lose their conviction and maybe a wiggle in the smoothness of Professor Gaster's line. This would suggest it is not only the angle of convergence, but the character of the line itself. What attribute is most defining, and which is most superfluous?

A better way to explain this is, 'At what point does a perception lose its reliability to carry your belief?' Even if you close the triangle, you might have three thin wobbly and errant lines angling the right way at the junctures but going haywire in the body or axon. Not straight. Or how about straight-angled lines that are cut short and don't necessarily touch. They strongly 'suggest' a triangle, but the wobbly lines do not. 'Not necessarily touching' or converging has its own implicit rules that our brains have decided on as specific to the language of shapes.

The degree of tolerance for deviation from those rules is fascinating. Most often, scientific cognition experiments deal with antiseptic paradigms to determine the speed of identifying them. Call that a reductive, barebones experiment. But the brain is probably working things out as much additively. Individuals should be tested even more often on increments of shape formation to see at what point recognition kicks in.

***

This is why it is virtually impossible to have a discussion about image-making without employing the concept of caricature, even for non-representation. This sounds counterintuitive or just outright inane, but a friend of mine paints nothing but fat lines as if she is trying to explain the world of linearity and she knows she is just skimming the surface. Another does skeletal white lines against a black ground to distill the barest truest most reliable shapes that portray the concept of house in the western hemisphere. How much of her representations are true enough to be universally understood? Is it the erect lines of the side against the horizontal, and could the Eskimos, with their round igloos, identify with it? Is this urgency for caricature the same thing that spurred Rainier Marie Rilke to make seventy-two poetic attempts, '*About a Panther*,' just to bundle the right attributes in the right configurations?

True, the word *caricature* has gotten a bad rap. It hasn't got the cachet of loftier terminology. You use it and people think of big noses and huge ears, of political cartoons, of comedy and jokes. But it is essential in the history of our cognitive record, the 'evidence of mind' as Owen Jones said in 1856. It is a cognitive process that exaggerates the basic attributes for expedient identification. It is the zigzag line on a cave wall in Southern France that a Cro-Magnon forbear enjoyed making, knowing full well that it exaggerated attribute of the bony back of a gazelle. There was very little extra he or she needed to add to get the point across. But there was a precise little extra something else. A zigzag alone would not have sufficed. In other words, what extra, tiny element in juxtaposition to this zigzag line did the artist know would constrain ambiguity?

Again, I call this syntax and it is as vital as verbal syntax. Would I go so far as Richard Leakey, Steven Pinker, and others have done regarding verbal semantics as a prerequisite for image-making? Hardly. It's ridiculous in fact. Though would I hang language on the coat tree of imagery?

Honestly, it's tempting.

***

Interestingly, it is often said that Autism spectrum deficits preclude this ability to caricaturize by selecting the wrong attributes because this disorder rejects salience. This condition tends to be a catchall for a number of clustered behaviors around a neuro-physical development early on, whereby the higher associative cortical areas do not adequately or normally connect with the frontal lobe. In her 2013 book with Richard Panek titled '*The Autistic Brain*,' Temple Grandin shows photographs of just this fMRI occlusion. Inevitably, autists select and harp on borderline associations that are easily expendable. Borderline as far as we think.

Borderline in our caricature library. Perhaps they have a different kind of dictionary.

Deficits in autism are typical for the language hubs of the brain, where the wrong characteristic or no particular effect is emphasized. Some extrapolate this to artistic savants, as did Oliver Sacks wherein their '...vision is valuable precisely because it conveys a wonderfully direct, un-conceptualized view of the world....,' the implication being that it is decidedly not creative. He suggests three more examples of this flat-lined creativity, that autist artists fixate on one thing, they do not take an ownership interest in finished work, and they do not tend to concentrate on their subjects while drawing. In other words, they don't seem to be emotionally invested in it.

In answer to these 'accusations,' I offer the following. First, regarding fixations, the artist Morandi just did bottles and Piranesi liked doing jig-sawed buildings. The list is virtually endless; the blue period for Picasso, houses for Hopper, squares for Mondrian, and flowers, just flowers, and never anything else for my favorite, Mary Delany in 18th-century England (Google her. She's a rare gem).

You cannot even begin to separate from this the nameless masses of artisans and craftsmen whose specialty has been one medium and subject matter for the duration of their lives. If you did, you'd have to eschew the entire repertoire of Moorish geniuses whose virtual obsession was their alphabet, that the Alhambra was a manic fixation of interwoven lines.

Second, regarding some outlandish formula that says artists must be possessive of their work, I suggest the research of Edmund Carpenter, who chronicled the passivity and non-possessive attitude of the Aivilik Inuits whose carvings and maps left their hands as fast as they made them, and without a parting glance. Perhaps even the Paleolithic artists might never have intended anyone to see their finished work, let alone even themselves after it was done. Then there's me. You. Anthropological records are replete with blasé attachments.

The fact is that our human record comes to us by way of this creative altruism. Many of us, myself included, like to sketch and just give it away or move on. We sketch while listening to a lecture, at a concert, having a conversation. Invested? Yes. But not as far as others can see. To others, it looks dispassionate and unserious. But it's deep inside our brains where it all happens, and we can simultaneously disport rather easily. So, am I autistic?

When we 'get it,' which can be a matter of seconds, we don't have to sweat the details and scrutinize the subject. For Stephen Wiltshire, the remarkable man whose early drawings of London are so well known, Oliver Sacks, in his book '*An Anthropologist on Mars*,' ventured into the realm of mind and symbols and intent.

'What power of reflective consciousness might be possible for him?' Sacks queries, baffled by the seeming nonchalance of this young man's creative moments as if that meant he had a less critical identity. I would suggest that for a little fun, sit in on a working session of illustrators. Their jargon is ripe, their hands flying as if on auto-drive as they sip coffee, listen to music, laugh, point, look up at the world, and maybe now and then down at the pad, all while they amazingly concoct something utterly keen.

Again, I caution those scientists who wish to tackle this top-down concept to tread lightly on definitions because the breadth of image-making is so far flung and profligate that 'art' is not explained so easily.

Were it that simple, why do we see so many spot-on autistic artists like Kevin Williams, whose work I collect? Kevin manages the most complex imagery, layer on layer of competing spatial devices. He has no problem selecting essential elements for emphasis (i.e., separating the merest kernels of wheat from the useless chaff). There is no visual or semantic ambiguity. This is very important to understand. What the world views as an image is what's left in the colander. 'Selection' is as much about that dynamic, negating process as it is the affirmative one that most people inflate. Kevin symbolizes and manages 'the caricature' just fine.

When speaking of art with respect to autists, many typically suggest that despite their enormous mimetic talents, they lack major creativity, and thereby marginalize their efforts. According to Beate Hermelin, '…though they [autistics] may have enormous talents, they are so lacking in subjectivity and inward-ness that major artistic creativity is beyond them.'

Inward-ness? How on earth could she or anyone know. Could she know *about* mine, is she a probe?

'Inward-ness' seems to be their non-social asylum, so I am unsure what is meant by this kind of description by a non-artist. But there does seem to be very well-documented proof that associative syntax is skewed. Either the linkage of sub-attributes is garbled or the data are too overwhelming to stabilize any kind of absolute identity. The latter has generally been the accepted theory.

If so, is it perhaps due in some aspect or other to a disconnect in the autistic brain between the afferent data and David Hume's 'necessary connection' of reliability based on experience. Perhaps from an ungated or differently gated flow of sensations? Temple Grandin, a highly visual and communicative autist explained it as a labyrinth of associations so intensely explicit and locked into autobiographical experience that you remain in the bottom-up world of parts and never synchronize anything into a theory of general attributes, though she seems to do so brilliantly regarding her slaughterhouse architectural blueprints.

I can't help wondering if this buffeting on a sea of turbulent and unending associations is in part the result of a physiological tsunami of afferent data, for example, from too many mechanoreceptors. And contrary to expectations, it is extremely worth noting that for many autists who have had no experience, they perform balancing skills like walking narrow gangways or even a tightrope as if they were born to it. Their proprioception is that remarkable and sharp, their gross motor mimetic abilities that acute, their navigational ability that self-centered.

Whatever discoveries lie waiting in the wings for this complex syndrome, one thing is certain, that the handling of objects hones our and their neural acumen for making caricatures, which are very much visual definitions. We share a commonality of expression and a standard for communication; in this case visual communication. Kevin, the autistic artist, is not scribbling. He is ciphering the same way I am when I paint or draw. This is despite the empty notion often coopted by well-intentioned outsiders looking in as to what 'art' is.

***

Isn't it curious that in my course on the Old Testament, Professor Gaster decided to use drawing terms to get his essential point across. He used to say, 'God didn't write the Bible with his little pinkie. He didn't draw man in his own image, we made Him.' Thus, it seemed most expedient for him to kick off this most frustrating topic, 'What is God?' with a sensible little icon. Thus, before completing it, he paused for dramatic effect. I remember him pursing his lips and impishly exaggerating the indent of his dimples. His fingers seemed clumsy around the chalk, which made it that much more memorable. I could feel the chalk in my own hand.

And as the true Thespian he was, he exaggerated everything by pulling that thin, wobbly, horrendously screeching line across the bottom to complete the triangle. In that moment he punctuated the entire mix of media for me; the mix of ideas, novelty, motion, touch, sounds, experience, imagery, and emotion, all through my ability to empathize with making this unique form.

It is a form so recognizable that it could yank a truly unique communicative moment from the inner seclusion of the now highly honored British artist, Stephen Wiltshire, whose Autism Oliver Sacks tried so gallantly to probe.

> Stephen's favorite building in San Francisco was the Trans-America Pyramid. When I asked him why, he said, 'Its shape,' and then with an uncertain air, 'It's a triangle, an isosceles triangle…I like that!'

Wiltshire has since been awarded in 2006 the Member of the Order of the British Empire and runs an art gallery in London. Thank goodness the rest of us can be awed by his intensity. He is specifically a caricaturist of scope and size enormity who uses cities and buildings to emphasize that theme. Over and over and over he works these caricatures out, just like Morandi did with bottles and Caravaggio with chiaroscuro.

*

Conclusion

It was a sweltering day in Tangier, Morocco. The 'Mosquitos' or tour guides to put it nicely, were swarming. I was ducking in and out of every little dark, deserted alley of the Kasbah, hoping to dodge their pursuit. As I ran past, I saw in a tiny cubicle, a man sitting on his knees, watching me, watching the traffic, hammering, chopping, and cutting colored glass for his excruciatingly beautiful mosaic, a pattern of diamond cuts and squares. A friend of his was there, smoking the hookah, sipping tea. But the visual and haptic story that fell into place beneath his knowing fingers, ah well….

The same is true of the Mexican ceramist painting his bowls while children scream, food is cooked, music blasts, tourists banter, and money is counted. Just because we are glib with our hands does not mean we isolate the moment in some beatific fashion. Image-making, okay, 'art' is to know 'about' by virtue of knowing what isn't. Onlookers think we work off some heightened inputting when in fact the trigger is 'ex-put', knowing what to shut out. Intellectual clutter is quite stimulating. If excising rather than collecting is the key here, then this explains our swift ability to sift out rather than include, a habit that is actually quite relaxing and self-determining. It becomes a matter of course, of habit, the process of which this book seeks to expose.

You can be sure we'll attempt to clarify some fuzzy areas of dismissive generalities that are overused regarding 'making art' by scholars and sages. Though well-meaning, they are generous in their praise for some, but exclude far too many in the so-called 'lower ranks' of image-making. This is because they tend to get caught up in the Humanist predisposition of the 'High' concept factor of Art as a derivative of Renaissance self-consciousness that has stuck like Krazy Glue to this day.

It's a context that has, I believe, obfuscated a clearer sighted view of image/object/art-making, particularly as it applies to people like Stephen Wiltshire, as Sacks described.

> Creativity has to do with an inner life - with the flow of new ideas and strong feelings.

This is a rather vapid comment when you stop to consider it fully. As such, I doubt any art critic, historian, or pedestrian would contest this, though they'd all disagree on their choices. Often, the Stephens and Kevins are charged with a deficit for the symbolic and abstract and a genius for *'concrete or mimetic representations.'*

> ...a sort of genius for catching the formal features, the structural logic, the style, the 'this-ness' (though not necessarily the meaning) of whatever he portrays.

Why are Wiltshire's panoramas of London, exploding with endless buildings, not a caricature of 'city,' which for him was an inundation of buildings? I am deeply confused. Why is that not a filtering for size and shape 'this-ness?' They were not Xerox copies, despite his having memorized so much in a twenty-minute fly over of the city. Stephen did not put everything in. In fact, he left most everything else out except buildings. He didn't select a crack in the sidewalk or an ant crawling up a lamppost, clouds, or people. In other work such as his depiction of historic sites, all have a very strong focal point, a tower or taller object, usually just off-center line, which emphasizes a point of view that directs you into the visual plane like any artist who knows his 'stuff.' Or a huge swathe of street or river.

He understands the language of the eye.

As for Stephen or Professor Gaster, it needn't have been a triangle except that it was their choice. That it was something useful to both of them, something similar, enabled 'it' to cut a swathe from the most intellectual and self-conscious like Gaster to ones who are often defined as trapped within themselves. Obviously, there is nothing superlative about this shape, nothing awesome. The world doesn't reduce to it and nor is it the one and only building block. Peace and hope don't reside in it, nor does perfection. I use it only the way Gaster and Stephen did, as a Theory of Mind and a platform of empathy, a common denominator constructed first from basic, shared sensations from the skin upward that formulate habits of thinking about things.

Cambridge, Mass.
2010/11

TRACKS OF MY FEARS

A curious thing happened several years ago during a rather dull banquet. I struck up a conversation with a retired physics professor who confessed that his great love was throwing pots and that he didn't care if they never saw the light of day. I understood how he felt, having long plied the art profession though being reluctant about displaying my work and often discarding it. Contrary to popular belief, creating imagery is not predicated on viewership. As reported to Robert A. Rundstrom in 1989 by an old Inuk Eskimo regarding the maps he had drawn from memory:

> ...he smiled and said that long ago he had thrown them away. It was the act of making them that was important, the recapitulation of environmental features, not the material objects themselves.[1]

However, one might think about the object once it is made, the driving force begins with an impulse for imaging, and this is the subject at hand.

We wondered through the evening about what triggers the human impulse for image-making, bearing in mind that it has no chokehold on representation nor on one medium over others. In fact, it might have nothing to do with media but rather only mind, and of course personality. Consider that a dancer carves a design out of the air with his arms and leaves a trace of that form in our short-term memories. We and they connect the individual moves into a fluid motion.

An artist crafts an image to anticipate a universal recollection by selecting salient associations that align with what others conceive. A musician captures our attention with hints of imminent notes such that we invent the next one just slightly before hearing it and then retrace the line by hitting mental 'replay.'

Unfortunately, though, these emanations of 'creativity' have been hampered by Western scholars whose awestruck exegesis has somehow removed them from the gamut of more humdrum human functions and set them high on a pedestal of enlightened inspiration. Given the 'Age of the Brain' in which we find ourselves, perhaps it is time to set this impulse firmly within the context of advantageous cognitive function. In other words, it is time to attribute the imaging impulse to the biology of our particular species, and one driven by decisive survival imperatives at that.

In each of the creative efforts mentioned above, we are led like Hansel and Gretel, with mere suggestions as to the intended route. One aspect of the 'event' is considered at a time, and in time, never altogether. And for each creative event, we move into it to move out of it. That sounds ridiculous, but it is true.

Figuring our way 'out' literally secretes our cognitive juices, and we do the same thing when conceiving or reading a piece of art. Clearly, we don't know where the whole dance is leading, nor the melody, nor can we for that matter perceive the entire wall of graffiti beyond the initial second before we automatically lock into a visual track to read the clues point to point (fig. 1).

All iconography and native design seems always to have careened toward complexity, asking us to stop short and follow the undulating line. A random sampling yields Maori canoe carvings (fig. 2), Celtic Knots, statuary folds, Belgian Lace, Yeseria-Moorish plaster work, Aztec serpent carvings, Labyrinths, apartment buildings, novels, and murder mysteries. You get the picture.

Why do we do this, and how does the artist know we shall succumb to the enticement of entering into their deceit? Because all these emanations depend on the willingness of the viewer to seek and follow a manipulated course, and instinctively collect these highly selected crumbs of perceptions like a path of escape through the forest.

But they are all nothing more than maps, especially when you understand that mapping is first about salient and fixed associations relative to each other (fig. 4). From these, one can plug in variable points of view or where one posits their attention, body, voice within that map so that only secondly is mapping about direction. All animals map their relative location by fixing coordinates.

Recent studies of the limbic system and hippocampus for rodents have isolated areas and neurons designated to plot such coordinates. They tend to make their way around their environment by distal plotting along the outer edge of their cages. It is assumed we are no different, a fact well established through the life story of Henry Gustav Molaison, now deceased, whose largely excised hippocampus still had enough tissue and the right kind to incise fresh apartment floor plans in his memory, though he couldn't recall his immediate past such as what he had just said or done minutes prior.

Our own antediluvian instinct to set down routes amidst a forest of pervasive ambiguity, and chaos is a driving biological habit formed by millions of evolutionary years in which our ancestors perfected erect bipedalism. We take it for granted, but our heritage is rooted in route-forging that is calibrated by the silent metronome of body functions like heartbeats and breathing, alongside the louder rhythms of stride, arm swing, and even grunts as we sight about thirty feet ahead, on average, to plot our own immediate path. This seems to be our natural, distal, sweet spot for foot navigation. Try crawling and you'll immediately see the difference in distal sighting. What our bodies naturally do - forms how our minds naturally mentalize the world.

It is therefore not surprising that our eyesight was standardized at around 20/20 feet. This can be tested anecdotally by anyone. Walk head on to an approaching pedestrian and note at what distance they swerve to avoid you. Try it, it's fun to do. Inevitably, they try to hold course, but angrily move off at approximately 20 to 25 feet. Their annoyance is often palpable, which itself is significant.

There is a great deal of information contained in this behavior, which informs much of our art thinking and application. For one thing, all visualization in this walking mode establishes an emphatic point of view. One's body—arms, hands, feet, nose, even torso—always frames out the periphery of our vision such that we never lose sight of ourselves. Repeat, never. Therefore, we navigate with a clear, though subliminal, perspective of egocentrism. And never, except for momentary stasis such as sitting or standing still from a high vantage and looking straight upward, does our vision ever free itself from the peripheral context of our physicality. Can you honestly say you have ever looked at anything without some indication of at least your nose in the field of vision?

***

In his book '*The Places in Between,*' Rory Stewart justified his trek through Afghanistan as:

> There was a magic in leaving a line of footprints stretching behind me across Asia...I watched the pebbles flashing past beneath me and felt that with each strike of each heel step I was marking Afghanistan.[2]

Marking the earth by stamping facsimiles of one's foot is something we discuss in later chapters. For the moment, let's just concentrate on the subtlety of the activity as it composes the way we think because the millions of years needed to evolve a truly erect bipedal creature did more than advance gross motor physiology; it helped organize the cognitive grid of our brains and the way we receive and dispense data. One's body drafts the connections between the coordinates—namely each step you take—as your mind calibrates all the various ways images get strung along in this highly structured and personal narrative.

In effect, the data coalesce around a natural grid created by the body's inborn measuring of pace. More than you think you know floods each step and fills out a given packet of data bracketed by your stride, meted by vital signs and sensorimotor processing. It's a reliable and orderly way of laying down information in minute narratives. Not just packets but of parentheses of information in a larger story that if scrutinized carefully are itty-bitty stories.

What brings them forward as essential recollections and ultimately as free-standing, cognitive or fabricated maps belongs to the way we triage caution. Which is why I entitled this chapter 'Tracks of My *Fears.*'

What's significant about the beginnings of 'art' as cautionary devices is that they map warnings so that for the first time, we could move forward and back in time to predict outcomes at the same time as reminding ourselves of momentous stories and what might happen should we not heed the maps we created a as warnings. We resurrect them, or aspects of them, as paradigms for our advantageous use in the future.

Let's just play a moment and suppose that at some point, Stewart's heel might have broken the ambient pattern of snow in conjunction to a gunshot. That fear elicited a search for environmental disruptions that would serve as clues to protect him in the future. On a biological level, we are talking about fear conditioning and regulating anxiety by being able to anticipate patterns. When you anticipate patterns, you can associate them or plug them in when available based on sensory inputs. This in turn modulates the activity of the amygdala.

Rather than superficial discussions of 'meaning' about art and design, and any type of behavioral routines, we are addressing something on a deeper, cellular level involving our 'archi' or ancient cortical complex of neurons called the 'almond' or amygdala. It is a cluster of cell structures better known as the amygdaloid complex where the basolateral amygdala is really the master modulator of fear and anxiety based on feeds from the thalamus, the hippocampus, and the cortex. Often referred to as our fight-or-flight hub, it is largely the reason we invent patterns to begin with.

Patterns are a form of classical conditioning always derived to countervail novelty. They are decisive collections of sameness, which implies a parallel and nether land collection of 'difference.' A culling process Stewart had to have sought and applied by noticing 'difference' as against 'sameness' for navigational markers in his narrative of fear and escape, which finally reached critical mass when fearing for his life. Fear being the key word here.

In lesions to the amygdala, patients can be receptive to visual prompts of faces with other emotions like happiness and sadness, even anger. But when it comes to mimicking fear, they draw a blank. Why does so much cellular content require fear processing and so little for other emotions? Before answering this strange deficit amidst other normalities, here's an even bigger finding.

First and rather obviously, the amygdala signals or synapses less when positive, 'valenced' stimuli are decreased, which makes a lot of sense.

Why bother getting all worked up about nothing? Furthermore, in a specific type of bilateral calcification of the amygdala, patients are able to identify emotions in all faces but for those displaying fear. It suggests that this particular neural cluster is exactly what we always felt it was—the fear/fright denominator.

An aside, however, is necessary. Your little dictionary of smartphone emoticons is not a great indicator of nuance. Renderings of facial fear is not a science; it is rather ambiguous. In fact, it is difficult to do without keying the facial contortion to a direct causal stimulus, like the presence of a huge spider somewhere in the format. A fearful face could just as easily be interpreted by some as a surprised or worried face among other subtle emotions. Anger is easy. We don't need to see the cause or trigger because the emotion comes from within and can often be a personality trait.

Now let's ask what happens if negatively charged or valenced stimuli are decreased, and not just for the patient with lesions but for all of us. The answer seems quite obvious.

Back to Stewart and the tracks he was laying down when he heard the gun shots. What if it were raining or blizzarding, and each step he took was completely obliterated in addition to all ambient traces of anything on the ground and around him? Perhaps it was barren of vegetation so there was nothing but a vast expanse of flat, patinated land of undiscernible marks.

To save his own life, he immediately needed to collect signs of difference that could be used as significant alarm criteria. But it was harder to do it now, harder to find and harder to think about. Harder to formulate patterns of normalcy and harder to figure out what was not. There was therefore, discontinuity between the expectation and foreshadowing of inevitable gunshots and the sounds. It would be harder to coalesce a fixed set of associations he could employ in the future against the unknown, whereas an irregular gash in the snow that he just passed would certainly be welcome. It could become his 'search alarm' for the presence of the Taliban.

It turns out that the amygdala, according to Michael Davis (2001) at Emory University, is;

> …especially sensitive to the uncertainty of stimulus contingencies…If one assumes that an ambiguous stimulus requires the brain to gather more information to decide to approach or avoid that stimulus, one can imagine that a system designed to promote vigilance and attention would show greater activation, the more ambiguous the stimulus. As suggested by Whalen (Paul J. of Dartmouth College) the fact that fearful faces are especially effective in activating the amygdala may reflect the inherent ambiguity of a fearful face, compared for example to an angry face.…

Something that is 'inevitable' means it is continuous. Something that shocks is the opposite. The amygdala channels information about discontinuity back to the neocortex where it combines other contextual data. Anxiety is a constant state of emotional discontinuity of expectations of shock due to the inability to accept reasoned evidence of expectations. If you can find the evidence of disruptions, you cannot be nearly as shocked or fearful.

And that evidence is present in the disruption of patterns (figs. 6, 7, and 8), which humans determined to be the primary indicator of environmental and emotional change, the essential emblem of significant stories. To this day, it helps explain why we instinctively scan repeats for the break in the pattern, and why J. M. Chernoff wisely wrote that there is power in rhythmic conflict precisely because, '…people are affected and moved.'[3] Or why Ernst Gombrich said,

> '…(it) contributed to an impression of rapid movement because we speed up scanning in an effort to grasp the visual array (fig. 5).'[4]

As we proceed, this quote will both plague and provide our goal. We'll mention it again and again. Or we'll imply it. It is the underlying structure for most of our inquiry. Think of it as a scouting expedition initiated by the amygdala. Ask yourself as you walk around, why do you even want to bother capturing a visual array in the first place? It must be awfully basic if our instinct is to scan so fast for irregularities. Or is it because we scan to establish the opposite, a nice, regular, safe pattern? You couldn't cross the street if you didn't do this, that is; scan forward and then scan back.

***

The 'art' impulse devolves from a similar forward and back referencing wherein Hansel and Gretel decide to leave the crumbs as a memento of their escape so that sinewy path becomes both the memory of danger as well as salvation. The emotional story of fearfulness, of being lost, of possibly being killed, validates the literal design of the path itself— as a 'search alarm.' Immediately it becomes employed either as a memory, but more usefully as a means of salvation and 'continuity' of expectations should they set foot in the forest again. In this way, we all enshrine salient associations to manage our environment. As an emblem, the sinewy path becomes just that—an icon of a sinew, a snaking line, a labyrinth, something by which we expect to find our way out and to which we are instinctively magnetized.

If I had a psychology lab, I would certainly conduct experiments on the amygdala reacting to designs such as these versus other forthright shapes.

***

Scientists are hard pressed to account for the 'imaging' latency and paltry record of our distant and apparently unbelievably lazy forbears. Were they bored or something, their fear neurons dead on arrival? Was nothing ambiguous, nothing surprising or shocking? Totally unlikely unless they were a pack of romping geniuses and we have deteriorated since.

So why *did* the Cro-Magnons wait over 100,000 years after our first documented appearance in Africa to produce imagery? A couple of repeated or converging lines would suffice as evidence, enough so that we could see they were thinking about their little visual map. And, yes, repetition absolutely is a form of master control and stamping a pattern against ambiguity. It's like the little crane being manipulated to make very distinct selections about the objects in their world.

Could this cognitive function have erupted in full bloom as many like Randall White at NYU believe, like Botticelli's 'Birth of Venus,' as something triggered by the societal changes and new requirements implicit in mass colonization? Well, we always were, and still are, colonizing. It's a matter of degree. A family moving is colonizing. A troop of extended families trekking across the savannah is colonization. A teenage Cro-Magnon pissed at his parents, and with a burning eagerness for the unknown, jumps on a raft and lets the waves take him somewhere new.

This is colonization too. So, what makes it critical mass and requisite for communicating across a larger and more complicated field of minds and bodies? Is it some critical number count of warm bodies?

Well, don't bloody believe it. Spontaneous, creative sophistication is about as plausible as a newborn singing 'la Vie en Rose.' Just think how hard it is to teach a child to draw a train. There are so many iterations of clumsiness and tentative facility such as just holding an implement that making marks and organizing them is altogether an extensive process.

Then take cave art, remarkable for having been sustained for nearly twenty thousand years, imagine 20,000 long, arduous years of rock and earth and clay. What iconography have we moderns ever sustained for that long? Why was the canonization of it (i.e., their stylistic lexicon) so steadfast and central to their lifeblood that it could endure thousands and thousands of years, likely as many years in the making beforehand, to formularize it in the first place?

Think of cave art or even Egyptian art as a tall skyscraper. To sustain it aloft and on solid footing, it needs a huge, deep cellar to support and anchor it. And in the same way, nothing from our brain is an *ex nihilo* event.

The plastic stability of objects, when viewed through the small end of a telescope, is misleading, the context for lives entirely lost and the natural dependence on the environment silent. It is important to remember that 'imaging' need never have been materially stable to function as art. Posterity has little to do with motive in this early impulsive stage, nor does identity and signing one's piece. As the art critic Sidney Tillim often warned us at Bennington College in Vermont, 'Don't be so precious about your work. Be willing to throw it away.' At which we cringed because of our efforts, but he was right. When you are willing to throw it away. you progress faster. Efficacy trumped durability.

In fact, until recently, mapping for the Aivilik Inuits in the arctic northwest territories of Greenland, Canada, and Alaska was about 'eye memory' first. Only eventually and perhaps reluctantly was it about transferring this paradigm of associations onto a plastic substance, the first one being the snow itself. According to Claudio Aporta (of Dalhousie University in Canada), breaking a land trail:

> …presupposes a deep knowledge of the terrain topography. They must know what certain landmarks look like when approached from a particular direction…know the wind directions…they must read the snowdrifts correctly.[5]

Friedrich Ratzel was among the first to use the term 'landmarks' about the natural geographers in Australia, whose arid lands and mercurial aquifers forced them to engage in extra thinking about markers. For others like the Marshall Islanders, whose survival depends on reading the nuance of their land, they configured a three-dimensional system of salient clues or markers that, according to H. de Hutorowicz in '*Maps of Primitive Peoples*,' remain undecipherable to this day and to our western eyes (fig. 3).

> They consist of wooden sticks fastened together at various angles with shells and small stones…The position of the sticks gives a variety of information, much of which is still obscure, but it is known that they indicate places where the combers fall most violently upon the shores.[6]

There is simply no other way to explain these maps as anything but sculpture, which begs the obvious question that all art is truly map making—formulating the essential relationships of salience such that it has steadfast readability among people sharing beliefs. These beliefs are the same as cognition, where the vagaries of circumstance cannot disrupt how we perceive difference.

For example, we have always needed to identify friends from foes in all light, twilight being the most problematic given the descent of the sun below the horizon and the diffusion of light. This causes a shift to rim lighting, of partial contours, and most importantly, the absence of shadow.

We needed to know that spots on a leopard at dawn were the same at noon. We needed to compensate for what Edwin Land described as retinex theory, wherein the mercurial perception of color in a changing context was cognitively discounted and color constancy intellectually maintained. We needed to know that for venomous snakes, 'red next to black, venom lacks, but red next to yellow kills a fellow,' even if the intense red looks gray in the red shift of evening. At some deep, cognitive level, we needed to construct a reliable code to safeguard us in all light.

How did we relate this wisdom? How did we pass it along just as we had to pass along which leaves were edible and which were poisonous?

To be frank, there is nothing different were I to draw the profile of a given face by plotting the distance between such markers as the nostril and upper lip or charting the inlet where the ear meets jaw. Thus, I am drawing a 'search alarm,' a system of attributes that will alert you to their identity by taking the guesswork and ambiguity out of our cognitive processing and letting the little amygdala take a breather.

An 'alarm,' however, is merely a warning to be constructively used, and does not come in tranches of bad or good. My husband carries fixed associations for my face that are so astronomically pervasive that asking him to describe it with the limitations of stringing one word after another is a mere specter of what he knows since he can find me instantly in a crowd.

Imagine being able to compare and then separate all the other configurations of noses and eyes and mouths and find the right one, and in mere seconds. And were there to be an emergency, that speed of recognition would be hyper-faster since the neural networking of the limbic system (our Paleo-brain including the thalamus, hippocampus, and amygdala) discounts ambiguity so fast that it seems simultaneous.

***

Walking is our gross motor form of delineation. It sets up narrative thinking by anchoring this form of cognition to one's personal point of view. This is key in our imaging behavior because it triggers a unique dialogue of 'self' versus the environment that is conceived as 'other.' This contrasts markedly with perception when we sit or stand with chin lifted forward and up as already stated as it is the only time we lose most of our body in our visual periphery.

Stasis has much to do with extreme distal viewing and the orphaning of our point of view. Looking up and out removes the bookended visual field of our physical self—hands, nose, etc.—and allows for panoramic surveying during which we lose our grounding of personal perspective. We become flooded with the fear and awe of a larger but unknown perspective in which we participate.

We become confused, lost. You may submit that these vistas are beautiful, but you feel tentative, small, unsure of your footing, and most importantly, you feel vulnerable. If we are so small, what might be larger; what do we look like to them or it?

Again, we are so used to this dichotomy of perspectives that we are little aware of the stealth effect it has on perception. It is doubtful, though unsubstantiated, that other animals are so buffeted by this point of view dilemma. Perhaps a reason is that we balance our head atop a spine without the weight of our jaws or brows pulling our glance downward, never freeing us of our own presence. The orifice through which it passes, called the Foramen Magnum, is positioned among apes in the rear, requiring strong nape or nucal muscles to hoist the chin up as well as it can.

Our species and only one other extinct relative sports such a central location for this connection, which according to Richard Leakey, might have had more to do with the shrinking of formerly massive brows and jaws as new cortical matter massed above the eyes. The upshot is that our neck muscles needed less power, allowing us to raise our chins and eyes. We now could look largely forward, outward and even upwards. Yet with this came a rude awakening. We finally had the choice to lose our body framed perspective and to float freely and seemingly unattached into the strange domain we inhabited.

In his book 'Thespis' on the origins of theatre, Theodore H. Gaster referred to this generalized natural stage on which we perform as the 'topocosm','the entire complex of any given locality conceived as a living organism.'[7] Thus, we get the terms for the anthropomorphizing of cities and towns as 'he' or 'she,' a behavior aptly described by John MacDonald in 'The Arctic Sky: Inuit Astronomy, Star Lore and Legend,' wherein the Inuits of Igloolik determine their enormously vital navigation routes across the ice as:

> ...the very arteries and nodes, the topographical
> anatomy, through which (they) comprehend the
> totality of their land and access its life-giving resources.[8]

Therefore, our perception of the environment is framed out by our individual physical body and personal relativity against an encompassing and projected point of view for this other being, the topocosm. Anthropologists call this a 'consubstantial relationship,' which is a very nice term, but does not adequately address the awe and angst of this ever-frustrating love affair.

Enter Augustine of Hippo, later beatified as Saint Augustine, but very much a man of the flesh and fully engaged in this battle of self versus the 'living entity,' and to such an extent, that it is to him we must attribute the word *soliloquy*. This is the specific dialogue among these various points of view, locked so deeply into our cognitive priming that some might even call it the source of our consciousness. But it is on this rich conflict that all imaging impulses and 'art' derive because those urgently required 'search alarms' were a personalized means for projecting the behavior of the topocosm.

***

On a very conscious level, the environment is a respected adversary. This has a lot to bring to our endurance behavior. For example, we mimic animals we intend to kill to infiltrate their routines. It directly increases our respect. Why wouldn't we do the same for the physical land we inhabit, particularly if we consider it both adversarial and essential?

How could we not extol the deer and dog paths we follow or the telltale lines of soft ice cracking? How could we not apply the patterns of interlocking vines and foliage for our weaving and knotting and building, or resurrect in our fashion the trees we climb, let alone all the beats, decibels, and movements that define this strange but all-encompassing organism?

And when we attempt to conscript these motifs for our beneficial use, we do it across cognitive platforms like playing three-dimensional checkers. We convert sound for image, touch for form, movement for pattern. Bruce Chatwin left Sotheby's UK to research this 'thinking' among the Warlpiri Aborigines. For them, 'Yiri,' or Songlines, best explain their mnemonic device for translating the topocosm into human terms. This is not about musical notes writ large, but sound as movement on a grand scale, conceived as footprint paths throughout their sacred lands. Seems complicated enough to me. But the following are the explanations, according to Chatwin, for their particular beliefs about con-substantiality. They are also known as 'dreamtime' myths.

> They believe that their land came into being as each
> ancestor scattered a trail of words and musical notes
> along the line of his or her footprints. This labyrinth of
> invisible pathways which meanders all over Australia is
> known as songlines....[9]

Art is as biological an imperative of our survival as is walking, procreation, and foraging because it has always been a cognitive thought test about triaging escape and success procedures against natural threats and for natural delights. It is a mental process first, which is then translated by the inherent clumsiness of one's limbs, of material, and tools and time. This includes intentionally dragging your toe in the sand or finger through ashes, things we certainly did for thousands of years before tackling stable media.

Given all these limitations, we must leave far more on the cognitive plate, far more information in our heads, than we can possibly hope to relate, thus forcing us to drill down hard and fashion the most effective map. 'I think I notice every bump along your chin but I can't draw two lines at once, something gets missed or forgotten. Nor can I speak two words at the same time. I discover, live, and create in analog and linear mode, and this requires me to prioritize.'

Contrary to Michael Polanyi's oft-quoted phrase, 'We know more than we can say,' suggesting that data operate as silent or tacit clues toward conscious goals, imaging or 'saying' it is truly the problem here. Siphoning the $10^{17\text{-}20}$ spikes or synaptic potentials in 0.5 milliseconds[10] of the human brain in a point to point configuring from which any cognitive transposition originates makes us momentarily *more* rather than less aware of those 'silent clues' simply because we can't use them all. 'Attending' means rationing to throttle down ambiguity. The good part is that we know it and adapt accordingly.

'Recollection' is an instantaneous process in this transfer. Because I shift my vision away from subject to drawing or from mind's eye to medium, I am in effect remembering and smudging all those minute connections. I am therefore deeply tracking associations to the exclusion of others.

But not all imaging morphs into art, nor are all 'alarms' worth remembering. We need to know about the cortical inroads carved by varying degrees of shock and salience. In other words, we need to know about the emotional impact of perception and why some stories, let's say about escape, are made to be remembered and others are merely place holders for ambient recollections, in the event of, say, ever passing Red Rooster Restaurant again for jumbo fries.

There is no answer, and never will be, a single explanation for why it is we do this or even how because we are an integrated network of so many moving parts just as we are the catchall of millions of years of primate evolution; a seemingly random but indefatigable experiment in adaptability. But the most telling evidence is that we responded differently to the environment because we were able to do so. We were endowed with the equipment that other species perhaps carried but we used best.

***

Erwin Schrödinger elegantly restates the 'use it or lose it' mantra when he explained in his essay on '*Mind and Matter,*' "Selection would be powerless in producing a new organ if selection were not aided all along by the organism's making appropriate use of it."[11]

We cringed and craved the unknown. Eskimos say, 'Glorious it is when wandering time is come.' In 1853, the French poet Theophile Gautier expressed the same thing in '*Wanderings in Spain,*' that the misfortune of modern life is the '...want of surprise and the absence of all adventure.'[12]

If our lives are primed by constant stimuli as are all creatures, we triage the cost/benefit of our responses to streamline the work of the day and expenditure of energy. We come to recognize that some 'shocks' are recurrent and non-threatening stimuli to be safely ignored. They are neutralized, in which case they are no longer really shocking. We call this habituation, and Eric Kandel has pointed out, that the synaptic permutations either erode or feather out marginally. He calls this homosynaptic depression '...because the synaptic response was decreased and homosynaptic because [it] occurred in the same neural pathway.'[13]

The take away is the characterization of the alarm or stimulus. 'Search alarms' were those categorizations of shock stimuli that had survival imperatives, most likely on a daily basis. In our peregrinations across threatening terrain, in our foraging and escape from predators, and in our delight with safety, succor and success, we triaged stimuli. Kandel calls this hetero-synaptic sensitization; 'It teaches the animal to attend and respond more vigorously to almost any stimulus after having been subjected to a threatening stimulus.' In this case, the neuron sprouts more connections to remember.

Classical conditioning is a more electric form of the same, wherein the coupled stimuli becomes the shock itself. I believe the imaging impulse derives from the sensitization category. 'Derives from' but is not so sustained because over time it becomes a pattern of habit.

***

Finally, we come to the art itself, the fixing of associations to be read across time and people. My only caveat is that our imaging impulse merely begins with search alarms; it is not the whole story. To tell that story, to transpose the choices, to literally get the idea out of the brain and physically configure the map of these stimuli, we needed something that most scholars consider to be the essential characteristic of speech.

Syntax is not the exclusive handmaiden of language. Nor is art the handmaiden of speech, leeching its structure and translating imagery into symbols, as many, including Oliver Sacks, Steven Pinker, and Richard Leakey, contend. 'Representation' is a restrictive drilling down of point to point selecting that must start and stop somewhere. Choices about importance and order, what comes first on down to last, is the means by which we 'convince' you of our map, specifically because we can't do two things at once.

We enhance this necessary order with parenthetical re-phrasings called recursion. There is simply no other way in our finite world, and it is in no way different than what Frank DeKova in the role of Chief Wild Eagle told 'F Troop.'

> Go back same trail you came. Make right turn at big
> rock look like bear and left turn at bear look like rock.[14]

This is about fixed relationships, with the added informational layer of personal relativity such that one 'knows about' salient markers in terms of oneself as the rogue coordinate. This is why terrain devoid of bold natural markers nudges passive 'seeing' to active 'looking.' and then contextual 'seeking.' R.C. Gagne explained this for the Eskimo language in '*Spatial Concepts in the Eskimo Language*' using the three-word sentence, 'ililavruk manna ilunga.' Translated, it becomes, 'Please put this slender thing over there crosswise on that end of that slender thing to which I am pointing.'[15]

Everything is relative. My Danbury Road is your Brewster Road.

Art depends on impactful sequencing, in other words, syntax.

And walking our way out of threatening terrain is our most basic conscious act of syntax.

In this same way, storytelling reveals itself as a progress set up by the thing we do most and better than other creatures. We walk in lines, alternating one foot after the other to get us from here to there, even as our thoughts dart around. But they too are sequenced just as our cognition is orchestrated by this sloth-like metronome. The memories we keep are insidiously keyed to it because we receive sensory inputs and configure thoughts that are laid down by means of the concatenation of our stepping. Just because we take this for granted does not mean it is not there. It is part of our biology, part of the way we input and arrange data to survive. Who hasn't said about forgetting something, 'Try to track it back.'

Some would say we are the supremely conscious creature. I'd say we are the supremely 'narrative' one. What matters to us and how we survive is pegged to the tracks we have laid down over thousands if not millions of years, our ancestors passing along the same metered walking that carved out unique pathways and habits in our brains.

We think and execute based on tracking that unfolds over time and incrementally. 'Search alarms' depend on this same syntax, associations that take precedence over others such that were they rearranged, the message could not be transferred and understood. I could not have drawn your nose above your eyes if I wanted you found. I could not have escaped the Taliban if I had not noticed my left foot stepping across someone else's track. This is a narrative as well as a map about escape crafted so as to be remembered with these salient elements crowding into each other. Our first search alarms required gravitas and utility, but that did not exclude irony and even whimsy as an effective means to demonstrate useful differences.

These inventions of ours were urgently felt and frustrating to execute as any artist can tell you. Even today, they aid us with remembering remarkable stories by becoming placeholders for them before eventually signifying them. Ultimately, when the urgency of the story recedes, the images become penumbral, mere shadows of their former function. So apparently for twenty thousand years, our ancestors never got blasé about their surroundings. Had they done so, the need for rendering the subject matter would have become hackneyed, merely a rote design and eventually a rather sloppy one at that.

Such 'art' evolves into the more commonly ascribed signage, metaphor, mementos, and icons. But it begins here, impulsively, desperately, joyously, seeking a path through the confounding mystery of the unknown.

Brooklyn, New York
2009/10

Notes:

1. Rundstrom, Robert A. (1990) A Cultural Interpretation of Inuit Man Accuracy, *American Geographical Review,* 80, 2:155-168

2. Stewart, Rory (2006) *The Places in Between,* (Harcourt, Mifflin San Diego, CA)

3. Chernoff, J. M. (1979) *African Rhythm and African Sensibility: Aesthetics and Social Action in African Musical Idioms* (Univ. of Chicago Press) p.160

4. Adams, Monni (1989) Beyond Symmetry in Middle African Design, *African Arts,* UCLA, 23,1:37

5. Aporta, Claudio, 'Routes, Trails and Tracks:Trail Breaking among the Inuit of Igllolik', *Centre Interuniversitaire d'Etudes et de Recherches Autochtones, Quebec*

6. Hutorowicz, H. De. (1911) 'Maps of Primitive Peoples', B*ulletin of the American Geographical Society* 43:669-79

7. Gaster, Theodore H. (1961) *Thespis,* Garden City, Anchor Press

8. MacDonald, John (2000) *The Arctic Sky: Inuit Astronomy, Star Lore and Legend,* The Royal Ontario Museum

9. Krause, Kerri Lee and O'Brien, Dan (2001) 'Adolescent Second Language Writers in China' Chapter 12 in *Research on Sociocultural Influences on Motivation and Learning* Ed. by McInerney & Van Etten

10. Many differ on this. It is also often quoted that we possess over 50 different types of neurons and perform over 20 million operations per second.

11. Schrodinger, Erwin (1992) *Mind and Matter'* (Cambridge Press, UK) p. 113

12. Gautier, Theophile (1853) *Wanderings in Spain,*

13. Kandel, Eric (2006) *In Search of Memory,* (WW Norton, New York)

14. *'F-Troop'* 1966, episode 19 directed by Gene Reynolds with Frank De Kova as Chief Wild Eagle

15. Gagne, R.C. (1968) 'Spatial Concepts in the Eskimo Language', Valentine and Vallee editors, *Eskimo of the Canadian Arctic,* Toronto, pp 30-38 Quoted by Judith Kleinfeld, 1971, in her study Visual Memory in Eskimo Children, *Canadian Journal of Native Education*, 11,3:134

16. Johnson, Kenneth O. (2001) 'The Roles and Functions of Cutaneous Mechanoreceptors' in *Current Opinion in Neurobiology* v. 11 no. 4:455-461p. Citation on page 458

17. Sacks, Oliver (1995) *An Anthropologist on Mars,* (Vintage Books, New York)

18. Hermelin, Beate (2001), *Bright Splinters of the Mind* (Kingsley Publishers, London and Philadelphia)

Figures:

1. Graffiti by *New York 79*

2. Carved wooden stern of 19th century Maori war canoe

3. 'Rebbelib' – Marshall Islands Stick Chart or map

4. Da Vinci's *Vitruvian Man* or *The Canon of Proportions*

5. Kuba Cloth, South Eastern Congo

6. Thar Desert (Great Indian Desert)

7. Tracks in the snow

8. Tundra Snow formations and patterns

1. Graffiti art, artist unknown, Red Hook, Brooklyn

2. Carved wooden stern of 19th century Maori war canoe

3. 'Rebbelib' Marshall Island stick chart of two island chains. It is believed that diagonals indicate waves and swells.

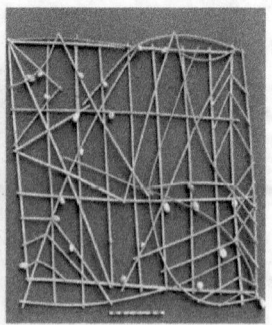

4. Da Vinci's Vitruvian Man.

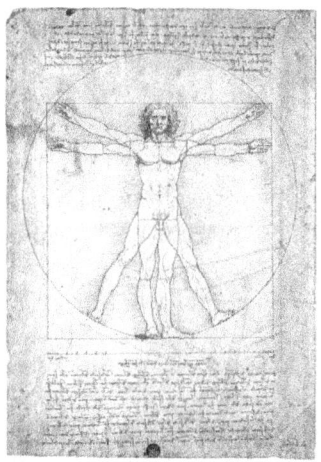

5. Kuba raffia cloth (short for Bakuba), Southeastern Congo

6. Thar Desert, Great Indian desert. 77,000 square miles between Indian River plain and Aravali Range and Punjab Plain.

7. Tracks in the snow.

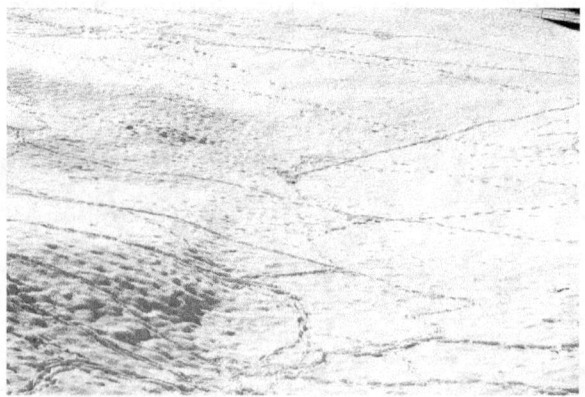

8. Tundra snow patterns

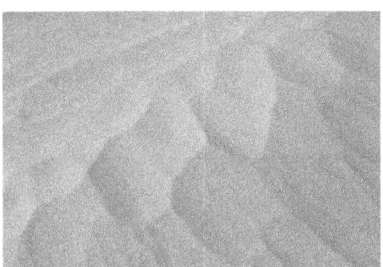

Bibliography:

Allman, John et al (2010) 'The Von Economo neurons in Fronto insular and anterior cingulate cortex in great apes and man', *Brain Structure Function,* 214:495-517

Allman, John et al (2005) 'Intuition and Autism: A possible role for Von Economo Neurons', *Trends in Cognitive Science* v. 9, i. 8:367-373

Arnheim, R. (1990) 'Perceptual aspects of art for the blind', *Journal of Aesthetic Education,* 24:57-65

Arnold, Derek et al (2007) 'Staying focused: A functional account of perceptual suppression during binocular rivalry' *Journal of Vision,* v. 7:7, Article 7

Arnold, Derek (2008) *'Perceived Size and Spatial Coding'* The *Journal of Neuroscience,* 4 June 2008, 28(23):5954-5958

Averbach, E. and Coriell, A. S. (1961) 'Short-Term Memory in Vision.' *Bell System Technical Journal,* 40: 309-328

Averbach, E. and Sperling, G. (1961) 'Short term storage of information in Vision', in *Information Theory,* ed. by Cherry. C., (Butterworth and Co., Wash. DC) pp. 196-211,

Arnold, Mathias (2004) *Henri de Toulouse Lautrec: The Theatre of Life,* (Taschen, Paris)

Baddeley, Alan (2000) 'Short term memory and working memory', Chapter 5 in *The Oxford Handbook of Memory ,* ed. by Endel Tulving and Fergus Craik, (Oxford Univ. Press)

Bainbridge, David, (2008) *Beyond the Zonules of Zinn,* (Harvard University Press, Cambridge)

Ball, Philip (2001) *Bright Earth,* Farrar, (Straus, Giroux, New York)

Baron-Cohen, Simon et al (2001) 'Theory of Mind in Normal Development and Autism' *Frisme,* 34:174-183

Baron-Cohen, Simon (1995) *'Mind Blindness: An essay on Autism and Theory of Mind,* (MIT Press, MA)

Baron-Cohen, Simon, Johnson et al (2013) 'Is synesthesia more common in autism?' *Molecular Autism,* Nov. 20th

Barret, H. Clark et al (2007) 'The hominid entry into the cognitive niche' chapter 25 in *The Evolution of Mind,* ed. By Gangsted and Simpson, (Guilford Press, New York)

Battaglia, Peter et al (2003) 'Bayesian integration of visual and auditory signals for spatial localization', *Journal of Optical Society of America,* v. 20: no.7:1391-8

Bednarik, R (1995) 'Concept Mediated marking in the Lower Paleolithic', *Current Anthropology,* 36:4:605-34

Berti, Anna and Frassinnetti, Francesca (2000) 'When Far Becomes Near: Remapping of Space by Tool Use' *Journal of Cognitive Science* v. 12, no. 3:415-420

Bickerton, Derek (1995) *Language and Human Behavior,* (Univ. of Washington Press)

Bickerton, Derek (1990) *Language and Species* (University of Chicago Press)

Bicknell, Peter. J. (1969) 'Democritus' Theory of Pre-cognition', Revue des Études Grecques v. 82 no. 391

Binkofski et al (2000) 'Broca's region sub-serves imagery of motion: A combined cytoarchitectonic and fMRI study' in *Human Brain Mapping* v. 11:4

Binkofsky, Ferdinand and Buccino, Giovanni (2004) 'Motor functions for the Broca's Region' in *Brain and Language* 84:362-369

Blaut, J. M. (1987) 'Notes Towards a Theory of Mapping Behavior', *Children's Environments Quarterly,* 4:27-34

Blaut, J.M. (1991) 'Natural Mapping', *Transactions of the Institute of British Geographers,* (The Royal Geographical Society, London) 16:2 pp. 55-74

Blaut, J., Stea, D. et al (2003) 'Mapping as a Cultural and Cognitive Universal' *Annals of the Association of American Geographers* , 93:1

Blazhenkova, Olesya and Kozhevnikov, Maria (2010) 'Visual-object ability: A new dimension of non-verbal intelligence,' *Cognition* 117(3):276-301

Botha, Rudolph (2010) 'On the Soundness of Inferring Modern Language from Symbolic Behavior', *Cambridge Archaeological Journal,* 20:3 pp. 345-56

Botha, R and Knight, Chris editors (2009) *The Prehistory of Language,* (Oxford University Press, UK)

Botvinick, Mathew M. et al (2004) 'Conflict monitoring and anterior cingulate cortex: an update', *Trends in Cognitive Science,* v. 8 no.12:539

Botha, R. and Knight, and Adams (1989) *Journal of Archaeological Method and Theory* September 2015, v. 22, i 3, pp. 952–979

Bril, Blandine et al (Jan. 2012) 'Functional Mastery of percussive technology in nut cracking and stone flaking actions...' *Philosophical Transactions of Royal Society,* v. 367, pp. 59-74

Brooks, Jessica and Cullen, Kathleen (2013) 'The Primate cerebellum selectively Encodes Unexpected Self Motion', *Current Biology:* v. 23 i. 11 pp. 947-955

Burkert, Walter (1974) 'Air -Imprints or Eidola: Democritus' 'Aetiology of Vision', Paper presented at *International Colloquium on Ancient Philosophy at Toledo*

Bush, George et al (June 2000) 'Cognitive and emotional influences in anterior cingulate cortex', *Trends in Cognitive Sciences* v.14:6

Buzsáki, György (2002) 'Theta Oscillation in the Hippocampus' *Neuron,* v. 33 i. 3:325-340

Bruce, Vicki and Young, Andy (1986) 'Understanding face recognition', *British Journal of Psychology,* 77:305-327

Caçola, Priscilla et al (2014) 'An age-related view of the role of object and spatial cognitive styles in distance estimating' *Journal of Cognitive Psychology* v. 26, no. 2:146-157

Caplovitz, Gideon et al (2008) 'Failures to see: Attentive Blank Stares revealed by change blindness', *Consciousness and Cognition* v. 17:877-886

Cardinali, Lucilla et al (2012) 'Grab an object with a tool and change your body: Tool use dependent changes of body representation for action' in. *Exp. Brain Res.* 218

Carter, Cameron S. et al (1998) 'The anterior cingulate cortex, error detection and the online monitoring of performance,' *Science,* v. 280:747

Cavanagh, Patrick (2005) 'The artist as neuroscientist' in *Nature:* v. 434:301-307

Cavanagh, Patrick et al, (2001) 'Attention based visual routines: Sprites', *Cognition* 80:47-60

Cavanagh, Patrick, Wang, Dina and Chao, Jessica 'Reflections in Art,' (Harvard Univ.)

Chao, Linda et al (1999) 'Attribute-based neural substrates in temporal cortex for perceiving and knowing about objects' in *Nature Neuroscience* 2:913-919

Clayton, Nicola et al (2007) 'Social cognition by food-caching corvids. The western scrub-jay as a natural psychologist' *Philosophical Transactions B of the Royal Society*

Corballis, Michael C. (2010) 'Did Language evolve before speech?' from *The Evolution of Human Language* edited by Richard Larson et al, (Cambridge University, UK)

Courtine, Gregoire and Schieppati, M. (2003) 'Human walking along a curved path…etc.' *European Journal of Neuroscience,*18:177-190

Critchley, Hugo D. (2004) 'Neural systems supporting interoceptive awareness', *Nature Neuroscience* v. 7 no. 2

Curtis, Rick (on line article on animal tracking) 12 pages www.ussartf.org/animal_tracking

Darwin, Charles (1872) '*The expression of the emotions in man and animals*' published by John Murray, London

Dawkins, Richard (1976) *The Selfish Gene,* (Oxford University Press, UK) See chapter 11, 'Memes: The New Replicators,'

Delagnes, Anne and Roche, Helen (2005) 'Late Pliocene hominid knapping skills: The case of Lokalalei 2C, West Turkana, Kenya', *Journal of Human Evolution,* v. 48 I:5:435-472

Doidge, Norman, (2007) *The Brain that Changes Itself,* (Penguin Books, New York)

Donald, Merlin, (2010) 'The Exographic Revolution: Neuropsychological Sequelae' in Malafouris L. & Renfrew, Colin, (eds.) *The Cognitive Life of Things: Recasting the boundaries of the mind.* (Cambridge, UK: McDonald Institute Monographs) pp. 71-79

Dugatkin, Alan, (2010) *The Imitation Factor; Evolution Beyond the Gene,* (The Free Press, New York)

Eichenbaum, Michael, (2014) 'Time cells in the hippocampus; a new dimension for mapping memories', *The National review of Neuroscience*, Nov.15(11):732-44

Evrard, Henry et al (2012) 'Von Economo neurons in the anterior Insula of the Macaque Monkey,' *Neuron* 74, 482-489

Faulstich, Paul, (2009) 'Comments: Notes on Memetics', *Rock Art Research,* 26:1

Fernando-Armesto, Felipe (2015) *A foot in the river,* Oxford University Press

Friston, Karl (2010) 'The free-energy principle: A unified brain theory?' *Nature Reviews/Neuroscience,* January 2010, online

Fragaszy, Dorothy (1998) 'How non-human primates use their hands' chapter 6 in T*he Psychobiology of the Hand,* ed, by Kevin Connolly (Mackeith Publishing, London)

Germine, Laura T., Duchaine, Bradley and Nakayama, Ken (2010) 'Where cognitive development and aging meet: Face learning ability peaks after age 30', *Cognition,*118.002:201-210

Gilbert, Richard and Weisel, Torsten (1989) 'Columnar specificity of intrinsic horizontal and corticocortical connections in the cat visual cortex,' *Journal of Neuroscience* 9(7)

Giovannelli, Joyce Lynne, (2006), *Face Processing Abilities in Children with Autism,* PH. D Thesis, University of Pittsburgh

Goldenberg, Georg (2002) 'Loss of visual imagery: Neuropsychological evidence in search for a theory' in 'Commentary/Pylyshyn: Mental Imagery in Search of a Theory', *Behavioral and Brain Sciences* 25:2

Goldenberg, G and Spatt, J. (2009) 'Neural basis of tool use', *Brain* v. 132 i. 6

Grandin, Temple (2013) *The Autistic Brain: Thinking across the spectrum*, (Houghton Mifflin Harcourt)

Graves, Austin R. et al (2012) 'Hippocampal Pyramidal Neurons Comprise two distinct cell types that are counter-modulated by metabotropic receptors' in *Neuron*, v. 76:776-789

Green, Marc, 'Night Vision' in *Visual Expert Human Factors* on line page

Griffin, I. C., & Nobre, A.C. (2003) 'Orienting attention to locations in internal representations'. *Journal of Cognitive Neuroscience* 15:1176-1194.

Gsell, Paul, (1971) 'Mystery in Art', *Rodin on Art*, (Horizon, New York) 1971 (171-181)

Haidle, Miriam N. (2010), 'Working Memory Capacity and the Evolution of modern cognitive potential: Implications from animal and early human tool use', *Current Anthropology*, 51:S1:149-166

Hardy, Arthur C. (1920) 'A study of the persistence of vision', *Psychology* of *PNAS* v. 6 p. 221

Hauber, Mark E. and Zuk, Marlene (2010), 'Social Influences on communication signals: From Honesty to exploitation' (chapter 8), in *Social Behavior: Genes, Ecology and Evolution*, ed. by Szekely, Tomas et al (Cambridge University Press, UK)

Hauk, Olaf, Johnsrude, I and Pulvermuller, F. (2004) 'Somatotopic representation of action words in the human motor and premotor cortex...' *Neuron* 41:301-307

Hauser, M. and Chomsky, N et al (2002) 'The Faculty of language: What is it, who has it and how did it evolve?' *Science* 298:1569-1579

Heiser, Marc et al (2003) 'The essential role of Broca's area in imitation' *European Journal of Neuroscience* v. 17:5

Hemming, John (2015) *Naturalists in Paradise; Wallace, Bates and Spruce in the Amazon*, (Thames and Hudson)

Higham, Thomas et al (2010) 'Chronology of the Grotte du Renne and implications for the context of ornaments and human remains within the Chatelperronian', *PNAS:* Nov. 107(47)

Higham, Thomas et al (2014) 'The timing and spatiotemporal patterning of Neanderthal disappearance', *Nature:* 512 i. 7514, pp. 306-309

Hikosaka, Okihide et al (2013) 'Why skill matters', *Trends in Cognitive Science* v. 17:9

Hochberg, Julian (1970) *In the Mind's Eye* edited by Mary Petersen et al (Oxford Univ.)

Hoffecker, John F. (2007) 'Representation and Recursion in the Archaeological record', *Journal of Archaeological Method and Theory*, published on line October 17th, 2007

Hölldobler, Bert (2010) 'Multi component signals in ant communication' in *Social Behavior* edited by Tomas Szekely et al, (Cambridge Univ.)

Hsieh, Po-Jang and Tse, Peter U. (2010) 'Brain reading of perceived color reveals a feature mixing mechanism underlying perceptual filling in cortical area VI', *Human Mapping*, (Wiley Liss Inc.)

Hubel, David (1986) 'Blobs and Color Vision', Cell Biochemistry and Biophysics', *Proc. Nat'l Acad. Science USA*, 9:1-2:91-102

Hubel, David and Weisel, T. (1965) 'Extent of recovery from the effects of visual deprivation in kittens, '*Journal of Neurophysiology*, 28:1060-72

Hunt, Amelia and Halper, Fred (2008) 'Disorganizing biological motion', *Journal of Vision* v. 12:1-5

Iacobini, Marco and Heiser, Marc et al (2003) 'Short communication: The essential role of Broca's Area in Imitation', *European Journal of Neuroscience*, 17:1123-1128

Ings, Simon, (2007) *A Natural History of Seeing*, (W.W. Norton, New York)

Istomin, Kirill V. and Dwyer, Mark J. (2009) 'Finding the way: A critical discussion of Anthropological theories of human spatial orientation with reference to reindeer herders of Northeastern Europe and Western Siberia', *Current Anthropology*, 50:1:5-28

Istomin, Kiril V. and Dwyer, M.J. (2008) 'Theories of Nomadic Movement: A New Theoretical Approach for Understanding the Movement Decisions of Nenets and Komi Reindeer Herders', *Human Ecology* 36:521

Jakab, Zolton (2003) 'Phenomenal Projection' *Psyche*, 9(04)

Jakab, Zolton (2003B) 'Why not color physicalism without absolutism?' Open peer commentary in *Color realism and Color Science* by Alex Byrne and David Hilbert (Cambridge Univ.)

Jones, Jonathan (2012) *Lost Battles,* (Knopf, New York)

Kandel, Eric (2006) *In Search of Memory*, (W.W. Norton, New York)

Kanwisher, Nancy and Yovel, Galit (2006) 'The fusiform face area: a cortical region specialized for the perception of faces' *Phil. Trans. R. Soc. B.* 361:2109–2128

Kawaura, Satoru, and Tachibanaki, Shuji (2012) 'Explaining the functional differences of rods versus cones', *Focus*, v. 1, Sept/October

Kessler, Klaus and Kiefer, Markus (2005) 'Disturbing visual working memory: Electrophysiological evidence for a role of the prefrontal cortex in recovery from interference,' *Cerebral Cortex,* (Oxford University Press), v. 15, i. 7:1075-1087

Kikyo, H et al (2002) 'Neural correlates for feeling of knowing: an fMRI parametric analysis' *Neuron* 26; 36(1):177-86.

Knoll, Max et al (Jan. 1962) 'Notes on the Spectroscopy of light patterns' *Journal of Analytical Psychology* v. 17 no.1

Koch, Christof and Tsuchiya, N. (2007) 'Attention and consciousness: Two distinct brain processes', *Trends in Cognitive Sciences* v. 11:1, 16-27

Kolb, Helga 'S-Cone pathways' in Webvision, webvision@hsc.utah.edu

Kozhevnikov, Maria et al (2007) 'Spatial visualization in physics problem solving', *Cognitive Sciences*:31, 549-579.
   (2013) 'Creativity, Visual abilities and visual cognitive styles' *British Journal of Educational Psychology* v. 83, i. 2:196-209

Kuratani, Shigeru (2005) 'Craniofacial development and the development of the vertebrates: The old problems on a new background', *Zoological Science*, 22:1-19

Landman, Rogier and Lamme, Victor (2001) 'Attention sheds no light on the origin of phenomenal experience', *Behavioral and Brain Sciences* 24(5)

Landman, Rogier (2002) 'Large capacity storage of integrated objects before change blindness', *Vision Research* 43 149-164

Lamm, Claus and Singer, Tania (2010) 'The Role of anterior insular cortex in social emotions' in *Brain Structures and Functions* 214:579

Lane, Nick (2000) 'Medical Constraints on the quantum mind', *Journal of the Royal Science of Medicine* v. 93:571-575

Lavin, Claudio et al (2013), 'The anterior cingulate cortex: an integrative hub for human socially-driven interactions', *Frontiers in Neuroscience,* 7:64

Leakey, Richard, (1993) *Origins Reconsidered*, (Random House, New York)

Levy, Daniel (2012) 'Towards an understanding of parietal mnemonic processes: some conceptual guideposts', *Integrative Neuroscience,* v. 6 i. 41

Libet, Benjamin (1985) 'Unconscious cerebral initiative and the role of conscious will in voluntary action', *Behavioral and Brain Sciences 8,* 529-566

Libet, Benjamin, Gleason, C. A., et al (1983). 'Time of conscious intention to act in relation to onset of cerebral activity (readiness- potential). The unconscious initiation of a freely voluntary act.' *Brain,* 106:623-642.

Livingstone, Margaret ((2008) *Vision and Art: The Biology of Seeing,* (Harry Abrams, New York)

Loizos, Caroline (2006 originally published 1967), 'Play Behavior in Higher Primates: A Review', in *Primate Ethology,* ed. by Desmond Morris, 176-218, (New Jersey)

Lynch, Gary and Granger, R. (2008) *Big Brain: The Origins and Future of Human Intelligence,* (Palgrave Macmillan Press, New York)

MacAnany, JJ and Levine, Michael (2004) 'The blanking phenomenon: A novel form of visual disappearance' *Vision Research*

Mamassian, Pasca (2008) 'Ambiguities and conventions in the perception of visual art' *Vision Research* 48:2143-2153

Marcellini, Sara et al (July 2010) 'A modified mark test for our own body recognition in pig tailed macaques', *Animal Cognition,* 13 (4), 631-639

Markovich, Slobodan (?) 'Amodal completion in visual perception' The *Journal* of *General Psychology,* 48, 113-132

Marsh, Lauren et al (2011) 'Disassociation of mirroring and mentalizing systems in autism', *Neuro-image* 30

Mather, George (2005) 'Two-stroke: A new illusion of visual motion based on the time course of neural responses in the human visual system' in *Vision Research,* v. 46 pp. 2015-2018

Matlin, Margaret (2004) *Cognition,* 6th edition, (Wiley)

Macleod, D. and Fine, I. (2001) 'Vision after early blindness', *Journal of Vision,* 1:3

McDonald, A. J. and Mascagni, F (1997) 'Projections of the lateral entorhinal cortex to the amygdala: a Phaseolus vulgaris leucoagglutinin study in the rat' in *Neuroscience* v. 77 I2:445-459

Makovsky, Tal and Jiang, Yuhong (2007) 'Distributing versus focusing attention in visual short-term memory' *Psychonomic Bulletin and Review* v. 14:6

Melcher, D. & Cavanagh, P. (2011) 'Pictorial cues in art and in visual perception'. Ch. 19. Francesca Bacci and David Melcher (Eds.), *Art and the senses,* (Oxford, UK: Oxford University Press), pp. 359-394

Merzenich, Michael (1983) 'The Reorganization of Somatosensory Cortex following peripheral nerve damage in adult and developing mammals' *Annual Review of Neuroscience* 6:32S-S6

Miller, J.A. (1987) 'Crazy Quilt Brain', *BioScience* 37:10:701-708

Miyake, Akira, Friedman et al (2002) 'How are visuospatial working memory, executive functioning and spatial abilities related? A latent variable analysis' in *Experimental Psychology: General* v. 130 no. 4

Murray, Micah et al, (2004) 'Setting Boundaries: Brain Dynamics of Modal and Amodal Illusory Shape Completion in Humans', *The Journal of Neuroscience,* August 4, 2004 24(31):6898 – 690

Nashner, Lewis (1985) 'Adaptation of human movement to altered environments,' *The Motor System in Neurobiology,* edited by Evarts, (Wise and Bousefield, Elsevier Bio Medical Press)

Nicholson, Philips T. and Firnhaber, R. Paul (2004) 'Auto hypnotic induction of sleep rhythm generates vision of light with form constant patterns' in *Shamansim in the Interdisciplinary context,* ed. by Leete and Firnahaber

Novak, Barbara (1980) *Nature and Culture* (Oxford Univ. Press)

Osaka, Naoyuki (2009) 'Walk related mimic words activate the extrastriate visual cortex in the human brain: An fMRI Study' *Behavioral Brain Research*, 198:186-189

Ostrovsky, Paul et al (2006) 'Vision Following Extended Congenital Blindness' *Psychological Science,* v. 17 no. 121009-1014

Oya, Hiroyuki et al (2002) 'Electrophysiological Responses in the Human Amygdala Discriminate Emotion Categories of Complex Visual Stimuli' *The Journal of Neuroscience,* 22(21): 9502-9512

Pardo, Jose V. et al (1990) 'The anterior cingulate cortex mediates processing selection in the Stroop attentional conflict paradigm', *Proceedings of the National Academy of Science*, v. 87:256-259

Passingham, Richard (2009) 'How good is the macaque monkey model of the human brain?', *Current Opinion in Neurobiology,* 19(1):6-11

Pinker, Steven, (2007) ' Toward a consilient study of literature', in *Philosophy and Literature,* v. 31, April:162-178

Pylyshyn, Zenon (2002) 'Mental imagery: In search of a theory' *Behavioral and Brain Sciences,* 25:157-238

Pylyshyn, Zenon (2003) ''Return of the mental image: Are there really pictures in the brain?' *Trends in Cognitive Science,* (Rutgers University)

Pryor, Francis, (2008) *Britain: B.C.,* (Harper Perennial)

Purves, Dale et al (2008) *Neuroscience,* (Sinauer Assocs., Sunderland, MA)

Quinn, J.G. (2008) 'Movement and visual coding: The structure of visuo-spatial working memory,' *Cognitive Processing*, v. 9, i. 1:35-43

Rabins, Peter (2013) *Seeking the Why of things* (Columbia Univ. Press)

Renfrew, Colin editor (2009) *Becoming Human, Innovation in Prehistoric Material and Spiritual Culture* (Cambridge University Press)

Rizzolatti, G. (1996) 'Premotor cortex and recognition of motor actions', *Cognitive Brain Research,* 131:41

Roe, Susan (2015) *In Montmartre: Picasso, Matisse and Modernism in Paris 1900-1910,* (Penguin, New York)

Ross, John et al (1997) 'Compression of Visual space before saccades' *Nature* v. 386:597-601

Russell, Richard, Duchaine, Bradley and Nakayama, Ken (2009) 'Super recognizers: People with extraordinary face recognition ability' *Psychonomic Bulletin and Review,* 16:2, pp. 252-257

Sacks, Oliver (1995) *An Anthropologist on Mars,* (Random House, New York)

Saygin, A. P. et al (2004) ' Point-light biological motion perception activates human promotor cortex', *The Journal of Neuroscience*, 24(27):6181-6188

Santos, Michael et al (2011) 'Von Economo neurons in Autism: A stereologic study of the front insular cortex in children', *Brain Research* 1380, 206-217

Schultz, Robert T. (2005) 'Developmental deficits in social perception in autism: the role of the amygdala and fusiform face area' in *International Journal of Developmental Neuroscience* v. 23:2-3:125-141

Seigel, Susannah (2010) *The Contents of visual experience,* (Oxford Univ. Press)

Seitz, Aaron R et al (2005) 'Visual experience can substantially alter critical flicker fusion thresholds' *Human Psychopharmacology Clinical and Experiment Journal* 20:55–60

Shipton, Ceri (2009) 'Imitation and Shared Intentionality in the Acheulean', *Cambridge Archaeological Journal,* 20:2 pp.197-210

Singh, Manish (2004) 'Modal and Amodal Completion Generate Different Shapes' *Psychological Science* v. 15:7

Smith, Denise (2009) 'Style vs Memetics: Exploring some new ideas', *Rock Art Research,* 26:1

Spruston, Nelson (2008) 'Pyramidal Neurons; Dendritic structure and Synaptic integration,' *Neuroscience,* v. 9

Suddendorf, Thomas et al (2009) 'Mental time traveling and the shaping of the human mind' *Philosophical Transactions of the Royal Society* 364:1317–1324

Sutherland, N.S. (1968) 'Outlines of a Theory of Visual Pattern Recognition in Animals and Man', *Proceedings B, The Royal Society,* 171, i. 1024

Studdert-Kennedy, Michael and Goldstein, Louis *'Launching Language: The Gestural Origin of Discrete Infinity* , (Yale University)

Thakkar, Katharine et al (2008) 'Response monitoring, repetitive behavior and anterior cingulate abnormalities in autism spectrum disorders', *Brain,* published by *Oxford Journals,* v. 131 i. 9(a) 2464-2478

Tallon-Baudry, Catherine et al (1999) 'Sustained and transient oscillatory responses in the gamma and beta bands in a visual short-term memory task in humans' *Visual Neuroscience,* (Cambridge University Press) v. 16:449-459

Thomson, Kaivo and Watt, Anthony (2013) 'Investigating cognitive styles differences in the perception of biological motion associated with visuo-spatial processing' *Polish Psychological Bulletin* v. 44(1) 50-55

Todorov, Alexander and Engell, Andrew (2008) 'The role of the amygdala in implicit evaluation of emotionally neutral faces' in *Social Cognitive and Affective Neuroscience* 3:4 303-312

Tomasello, Michael (1999) *The Cultural Origins of Human Cognition* (Harvard University Press, Cambridge)

Tse, Peter Ulrich (1999a) 'Volume Completion', *Cognitive Psychology* 39:37-68 (1999b) 'Complete mergeability and amodal completion' in *Acta Psychologica* 102:165-201

Turner, Jonathan H. and Maryanski, Alexandra (2008) *On the Origin of Societies by Natural Selection,* (Paradigm, London)

Ullsperger, Markus et al (2014) 'Neurophysiology of performance monitoring and adaptive behavior', v. 94 no. 1, 35-79

Ungerleider, Leslie G. et al (1998), 'A neural system for human visual working memory', *Proc. National Acad. of Sciences USA,* 95:3:883-890

Vaina, Lucia and Solomon, J et al (2001) 'Functional Neuroanatomy of Biological Motion Perception in Humans', *PNAS,* (Sept.) 98:20

Valentine, Tim (1991) 'A Unified account of the effects of distinctiveness, inversion and race in face recognition', *Quarterly Journal of Experimental Psychology,* 43A:2:161-204)

Von Humboldt, Wilhelm (1999) *On Language, On the Diversity of Human Language Construction and its Influence on the Mental Development of the Human Species.* Edited by Michael Losonsky, pp. 25-64

Wade, Nicholas and Brozek, J. (2006) *Purkinje's Vision,* Lawrence Erlbaum, London

Wallace, Alfred Russell (1858 - July) 'On the tendencies of varieties to depart indefinitely from the original type' (The Ternate Essay) from the *Linnean Society Proceedings of London,* v. 3

Wallis, T. S. A. and Bex, P.J. (2011) 'Visual crowding is correlated with awareness' *Current Biology,* Feb. 8; 21(3):254–258.

Wallis, T and Arnold, D. (2008) 'Motion-induced blindness is not tuned to retinal speed' *Journal of Vision,* February v. 8 no. 2 article 11

Watson, Karli (2006) '*The Von Economo Neurons: From cells to behavior*' Doctoral Thesis for Cal Tech.

Watson, K.K. et al (2006) 'Dendritic architecture of Von Economo neurons', *Neuroscience,*141:1107-1112

White, Randall (1992) 'Towards an Understanding of Material Representation in Western Europe' *Annual Review of Anthropology,* 21:537-564

White, Randall (2006-2007) *Prehistoric Art,* Lecture Series at New York University

Whiten, A. Goodall, J. et al (2001) 'Charting cultural variation in chimpanzees' in *Behavior*

Williams, Justin (2008) 'Self other relations in social development and autism: multiple roles for mirror neurons and brain bases' in *Autism Research,* v.1 i. 2

Wood, Chip (1997) *Yardsticks,* (Northeast Foundation for Children, Greenfield, MA)

Wolpert, DM and Flannigan, JR (2010)'Motor Learning' *Current Biology* 8;20(11):467-72.

Wyder, Melanie T. (2004), 'Contextual Modulation of Central Thalamic Delay Period Activity: Representation of Visual and Saccadic Goals', *Journal of Neurophysiology,* 91:2628-2648

Xu, Yaoda and Jeong, Su Keun (2015) 'The contribution of human superior intraparietal sulcus to visual short-term memory and perception,' Chapter 4 in *Mechanisms of Sensory Working Memory* edited by Pierre Jolicouer et al, (Elsevier Press)

Xu, Yaoda (2007) 'The role of the superior intraparietal sulcus in supporting visual short-term memory for multifeatured objects', *Journal of Neuroscience,* v. 27 i. 43

Zimmer, Hubert D. (2008) 'Visual and spatial working memory: From boxes to networks', *Neuroscience and Behavioral Reviews* v. 32:1373-1395

Index

A

abilities
  cognitive, 30
  navigational, 50, 83
  swift, 52
Acheulean, 85
Agnosia, verbal, 45
alarms as triaged stimuli, 68
Alaska
  Aivilik Inuits, 48, 62, 65, 71
  Aporta, Claudio also, 62, 71
  Eskimo Language, 47, 67, 69, 72
  eye memory, 62
Alhambra, 48
ambient patterns, 57, 59
ambiguity, 35, 40, 59, 61, 67
amodal completion, 83, 85
amygdala
  bilateral calcification, 58
anterior cingulate cortex, 22, 41–42, 78–80, 82, 84–85
anticipation
  distal goals, 25–28, 34
  intellectual, 26
  regulating anxiety, 57
Aporta, Claudio also. *See under* Alaska
artify, 33. *Also see under* Dissanayake
Augustine of Hippo, 65
Australia, 62, 66
autists, 19, 23–24, 48–50, 81
Aztec serpent carvings, 55

B

Belgian Lace, 55
beta and gamma bands, 85
blindness, 25, 83

I

K

L